P9-CTQ-975

CHANGING ASPECTS OF URBAN RELIEF

A Da Capo Press Reprint Series

FRANKLIN D. ROOSEVELT
AND THE ERA OF THE NEW DEAL
GENERAL EDITOR: FRANK FREIDEL
Harvard University

[U.S. _York Projects Administration_ (handwritten)]

CHANGING ASPECTS
OF URBAN RELIEF

By

F. L. Carmichael

and

R. Nassimbene

ST. JOSEPH'S UNIVERSITY   STX
HV85.A53 1974
Changing aspects of urban relief,

3 9353 00154 8930

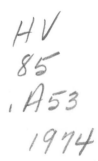

HV
85
.A53
1974

155925

DA CAPO PRESS · NEW YORK · 1974

Library of Congress Cataloging in Publication Data

U. S. Work Projects Administration.
  Changing aspects of urban relief.

  (Franklin D. Roosevelt and the era of the New Deal)
  Reprint of the 1939 ed.
  1. Unemployed—United States. 2. Work relief—United States. I. Carmichael,
Fitzhugh Lee, 1893- II. Nassimbene, Raymond. III. Title. IV. Series.
HV85.A53   1974b   362.8'5   72-173446
ISBN 0-306-70370-X

This Da Capo Press edition of *Changing Aspects of Urban Relief* is an
unabridged republication of the 1939 edition published in Washington, D.C.
It is reprinted from a copy in the collections of the Cleveland Public Library.

Published by Da Capo Press, Inc.
A Subsidiary of Plenum Publishing Corporation
227 West 17th Street, New York, N.Y. 10011

All Rights Reserved

Manufactured in the United States of America

CHANGING ASPECTS OF URBAN RELIEF

WORKS PROGRESS ADMINISTRATION

F. C. Harrington, *Administrator*

Corrington Gill, *Assistant Administrator*

DIVISION OF RESEARCH

Howard B. Myers, *Director*

CHANGING ASPECTS OF URBAN RELIEF

By

F. L. Carmichael

and

R. Nassimbene

Under the supervision of
John N. Webb
Chief, Urban Surveys Section
Division of Research

•

1939

UNITED STATES GOVERNMENT PRINTING OFFICE, WASHINGTON

PREFACE

A SURVEY of changing aspects of the urban relief population was made in 1935, in a sample of 13 cities, by the Division of Research, Statistics, and Finance, of the Federal Emergency Relief Administration. Several bulletins have been published as a result of the survey. However, the statistical data as a whole have not been made available. This report presents these data for the entire year along with a brief topical analysis indicating the principal findings of the study. The report was prepared in the Division of Research, Works Progress Administration, by F. L. Carmichael and R. Nassimbene, under the supervision of John N. Webb, Coordinator of Urban Research. Special acknowledgment is made of the contribution of John W. Mitchell who collaborated in the preparation of the tabular material, Charles H. Wagner who supervised the editing of the schedules and the tabulation of the data, and Mary Parker Ragatz who edited the report.

Contents

FIGURES

Changing Aspects of Urban Relief

INTRODUCTION

AS THE Works Program becomes more generally recognized as an efficient method of assisting the unemployed, there is danger that some of the salient features of Federal participation in direct relief under the Federal Emergency Relief Administration may be obscured. Proposals for a return to direct relief recur so persistently that the experiences of the years 1933 to 1935 have much more than a historical interest.

This report does not attempt an evaluation of direct relief. Nor does it cover the entire period during which direct relief was the principal form of assistance. Instead, it attempts the much less ambitious task of describing the operation of direct relief in a representative sample of 13 cities during the year 1935 when the transfer from direct relief to the Works Program was made. The data presented are drawn from studies made during 1935 for the purpose of describing the changing aspects of urban relief. For specific months and on specific topics the results of these studies have already been published,[1] but the results

---

[1] Division of Research, Statistics, and Finance, *The Relief Turnover in 13 Cities, January 1935,* Research Bulletin Series I, No. 5, Federal Emergency Relief Administration, Washington, D. C., May 16, 1935.

Division of Research, Statistics, and Finance, *Current Changes in the Urban Relief Population, February 1935,* Research Bulletin Series I, No. 7, Federal Emergency Relief Administration, Washington, D. C., June 22, 1935.

Division of Research, Statistics, and Finance, *Current Changes in the Urban Relief Population, March 1935,* Research Bulletin Series I, No. 8, Federal Emergency Relief Administration, Washington, D. C., August 22, 1935.

Mueller, John H., *Current Changes in the Urban Relief Population, April 1935,* Research Bulletin Series I, No. 10, Division of Research, Statistics, and Finance, Federal Emergency Relief Administration, Washington, D. C., September 21, 1935.

Carmichael, F. L. and Coe, Paul F., *Current Changes in the Urban Relief Population, May 1935,* Research Bulletin Series I, No. 12, Division of Research, Statistics, and Finance, Federal Emergency Relief Administration, Washington, D. C., October 21, 1935.

Carmichael, F. L. and Mitchell, John W., *Current Changes in the Urban Relief Population, June—July 1935: Trend of Employable Persons on Relief in 13 Cities by Industrial Groups,* Research Bulletin Series I, No. 14, Division of Research, Statistics, and Finance, Federal Emergency Relief Administration, Washington, D. C., November 20, 1935.

Carmichael, F. L. and Mitchell, John W., *Current Changes in the Urban Relief Population, August 1935: Trend of Employable Persons on Relief in 13 Cities by Occupational Groups,* Research Bulletin Series I, No. 17,

for the entire year and for the full range of topics are brought together in this bulletin for the first time.

The more important facts about relief cases, persons, and workers are presented in simple topical form. Appendix tables support the text discussion. The report does not attempt an exhaustive analysis of these facts. When time has brought perspective and a fuller understanding of the problem of unemployment and relief, it will be possible to write a fully integrated story of the period of direct relief. When that time comes the present report should be of considerable assistance.

For ready reference the sections of this report are arranged under broad headings pertaining to the following subjects: proportion of the population receiving relief or wage assistance; trends of the relief and wage assistance load; accession and separation rates; reasons for opening and closing relief cases; occupational and industrial shifts of experienced workers; supplementation of private-employment earnings with relief; unemployment duration and reemployment; and transfers to the Works Program.

Sufficient detail is presented under each heading to show variations according to the personal and economic characteristics of the recipients of assistance. Liberal use has been made of subheadings both to permit easy reference and to simplify the task of putting together such a large mass of material in readable form. Tables supporting the text statements are to be found in the statistical appendix.

The 13 cities selected for the survey were: Atlanta, Ga.; Baltimore, Md.; Bridgeport, Conn.; Butte, Mont.; Chicago, Ill.; Detroit, Mich.; Houston, Tex.; Manchester, N. H.; Omaha, Nebr.; Paterson, N. J.; St. Louis, Mo.; San Francisco, Calif.; and Wilkes-Barre, Pa. These cities are drawn from widely separated sections of the country; both large and small cities are included among them, and every major industry of the country is represented in at least 1 of the 13. Some industries—notably automobile manufacturing—are overrepresented; mineral extraction and textile manufacturing are underrepresented. Because of the importance of the Negro population in most of the large cities included in the survey, there is overrepresentation of Negroes. However, statistical tests show that the relief population of these cities is generally representative of the total urban relief population in respect to age, sex, and occupational background.

Division of Social Research, Works Progress Administration, Washington, D. C., January 15, 1936.

Carmichael, F. L. and Nassimbene, Raymond, *Unemployable Relief Cases in 13 Selected Cities*, Research Bulletin Series I, No. 19, Division of Social Research, Works Progress Administration, Washington, D. C., May 6, 1936.

CHANGING ASPECTS OF URBAN RELIEF

PROPORTION OF THE GENERAL POPULATION IN 13 CITIES RECEIVING RELIEF OR WAGE ASSISTANCE DURING 1935

THE RELIEF population may be described in terms of three different units. If the interest is in the general characteristics of all persons in the relief population, the relief *person* is the proper unit of study; if the primary interest is in the family as the relief unit, then attention is focused upon the relief *case;* and if the interest is in those persons who are either working or seeking work, the relief *worker* is the unit for study. In the present chapter analysis and discussion are presented in terms of each of these three units.[1]

The general population of the 13 cities in 1935 was estimated at 9,104,000 persons.[2] Of this number 1,276,600 or 14 percent were on the relief rolls in December 1934. During the year 218,000 persons, constituting 2 percent of the inhabitants of these cities, received relief for the first time[3] (appendix table 1). An estimated additional 2 percent had received relief prior to 1935 and were readmitted to the relief registers during the year. If these 2 groups be added to the 14 percent on relief in the 13 cities in December 1934, it may be seen that about 18 percent of the population received relief at some time within the 13-month period December 1934 through December 1935.

For urban United States as a whole there were an estimated 11,400,000 persons receiving relief in December 1934 or about

---

[1]A relief *case* consists of one or more related or unrelated persons living together, receiving aid as one unit, and considered as one case by the agency giving this aid. *Persons* include all members of cases. *Workers* comprise all members 16—64 years of age, inclusive, either working or seeking work.

[2]General population estimate for the 13 cities as of July 1, 1935. The method of making the 13-city estimates is that set forth in the release of the Bureau of the Census, *Estimated Population of the United States as of July 1, 1935,* U. S. Department of Commerce, Washington, D. C., February 12, 1936.

[3]That is, for the first time in the city from which the registration was reported. Approximately one-sixth of these new cases had received relief in some other city. See p. 13.

16 percent of the total urban population.[4] If the number of persons admitted for the first time to relief, plus those re-admitted in 1935, were proportionately as large for all the urban areas as for the 13 cities studied, then about 20 percent of the population of urban United States received relief at some time in 1935.

In summary, therefore, the total number of different persons receiving relief at some time in 1935 in the 13 cities was greater than the number actually on relief in December 1934, but the actual number of persons receiving relief or wage assistance was smaller at the end than at the beginning of the year. The decline in the number of persons receiving relief or wage as-sistance in the 13 cities was from 14.0 percent of the popula-tion in December 1934 to 12.5 percent in December 1935 (appendix table 2).

Proportion of Persons Receiving Relief or Wage Assistance

Proportion by Age Groups

The median age of all persons receiving aid was 24 years, while the median for the general population was 30 years. This dif-ference of 6 years was due to the large number of children among families on relief. Children under 16 in cases receiving re-lief or wage assistance in December 1935 constituted almost a fifth of all children under 16 in the general population, where-as among other age groups the proportions of the population were considerably smaller. The proportion of the population receiving aid was somewhat smaller for the group 65 and over than for the group 45—64 years of age partly because of provisions for the aged through pensions and institutions.

Proportion by Sex

Approximately the same proportions of the men and women in the general population received aid at the beginning and end of 1935: about 14 percent of each sex received aid in December 1934 and 12.5 percent received aid in December 1935 (appendix table 2).

Proportion by Race

The proportion of the Negro population receiving aid was three times that of whites among all age groups under 65 years, both in December 1934 and in December 1935. Approximately a third of all Negroes and a ninth of all whites received aid at the beginning of the year, while for both races the proportions re-ceiving aid were somewhat smaller at the end of the year. Among

---

[4]Urban relief population estimate of 11,400,000 persons as of December 1934 and total general population estimate of 71,000,000 as of January 1, 1935, made by Urban Estimates Section, Division of Social Research, Works Progress Administration, Washington, D. C.

Negroes about a half of the children under 16 years and almost a half of the age group 65 and over were on the rolls. The greater representation of Negro than of white population on relief was particularly marked in the age group 65 years and over, where the proportion of Negroes was five times that of whites. This racial difference may be attributed in the main to two factors. First, the resources upon which aged Negroes can draw are less than those of aged whites (appendix table 2). And second, unskilled persons—a predominant group among Negroes—find age a greater handicap in securing employment than do other occupational groups.

The proportion of Negroes first admitted to relief in 1935 was about twice that of whites for each age group except the group 65 and over. For this oldest group the proportion for Negroes was over three times that for whites (appendix table 1).

Proportion of Families Receiving Relief or Wage Assistance
Proportion by Size of Family[5]

The proportion of large families in the general population receiving aid was markedly greater than that of small families. Less than a seventh of all two-person families in the general population were on relief both in December 1934 and in December 1935. At the other extreme, the proportion of families of 10 persons or more was nearly a fourth at the beginning of the year and slightly over a fifth at the end (fig. 1 and appendix table 3).

Proportion of Experienced Workers Receiving Relief or Wage Assistance
Proportion by Socio-Economic Groups

In December 1934 about a tenth of all experienced workers in the 13 cities were receiving relief or wage assistance. The proportion was lowest in the white-collar group and highest in the unskilled group. In the latter group the proportion of

---

[5]The number of unattached individuals in the general population is not available from the reports of the U. S. Bureau of the Census. It is necessary, therefore, to exclude one-person cases and to limit the study of relief incidence by size of case to family cases.

Reports of the Census Bureau for 1930 show that 10 percent of the people in the 13 cities were either lodgers or members of so-called "quasi families," the latter consisting largely of people living in hotels and rooming houses. Inasmuch as census family data are reported only for the remaining 90 percent of the population, such family-size data are understatements of the number of families of various sizes in the general population.

While census data are not available on the distribution of lodgers and quasi families, by family units of various sizes, it is doubtless true that the bulk of them consists of the smaller units, especially one-person cases, and that the understatement of families in the general population, referred to in the preceding paragraph, is relatively greater in the families of small size than in the families of large size. It follows, therefore, that the proportion of small families receiving relief or wage assistance is overstated in fig. 1 to a greater extent than the proportion of large families.

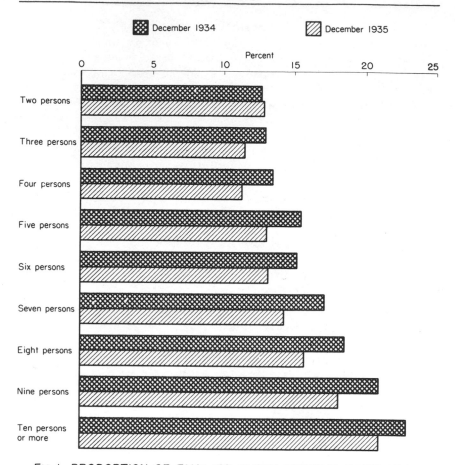

FIG. I - PROPORTION OF FAMILIES IN THE GENERAL POPULATION
RECEIVING RELIEF OR WAGE ASSISTANCE
BY SIZE OF CASE, 13 CITIES
December 1934 and December 1935

Source: Table 3.

AF-3002, WPA

manual laborers receiving aid was considerably below that of
domestic and personal service workers. The proportions for the
different groups are shown in appendix table 4.

Approximately 2.1 percent of the experienced workers in the
13-city population received their first relief in 1935. Among
the occupational groups the proportion was lowest for the white-
collar group, and it was only slightly higher for skilled workers.
This may be due in part to the greater resources upon which
these groups can draw after losing their jobs. The proportions
were considerably higher for semiskilled workers and for unskilled workers, the latter being the highest. Among unskilled
workers the proportion of laborers receiving first relief in

1935 was considerably below that of domestic and personal service workers.[6]

Proportion by Usual Industry

The proportion of workers receiving aid in December 1934 was greater in the building industry than in other industries. The proportion was nearly as high in the domestic group and only slightly less in the food group.[7] It was lowest in the trade group.

By far the greatest change during 1935 occurred in the automobile group, where the proportion of workers receiving aid dropped about a half in December 1935. The rapid revival in this industry and the early appearance of the 1936 automobile models undoubtedly were responsible (appendix table 5).

TRENDS OF THE RELIEF AND WAGE ASSISTANCE LOAD IN 13 CITIES DURING 1935

An increase or decrease in the number of cases receiving aid[8] was, in general, paralleled by a similar increase or decrease in the number of persons and of workers. But the amount of increase or decrease among these three groups was not always proportionate. For example, from December 1934 to December 1935 the relief and wage assistance case load declined 6 percent, the number of persons in these cases fell 11 percent, and the number of workers in receipt of aid declined 8 percent (appendix table 6).

Trend of Relief and Wage Assistance to Persons

Trend by Age Groups

The largest declines in the number of persons receiving aid were in the younger age groups. Between the beginning and end of 1935 the number of persons receiving aid in the three younger age groups (under 16, 16—24, and 25—44 years) declined between 12 and 13 percent. During the same period, however, the number of persons receiving aid in the age group 45—64 years declined only 5 percent and the number in the group 65 years of age and over remained about the same (appendix table 7).

These changes necessarily affected the age distribution of persons receiving aid. During the year two of the younger age groups (16—24 and 25—44 years) steadily declined in relative importance, while the two older age groups (45—64 and 65 years

---

[6]From unpublished data in the files of the Division of Research.

[7]The incidence of aid in the food group is considered larger than the food-group average for the country. This conclusion is based upon an examination of 1930 Census data showing that slaughtering and meat packing, which suffered severe employment declines in the latter part of 1934 and 1935, constitutes a far greater proportion of the food-group total for 13 cities than for the country as a whole.

[8]The terms *aid* and *relief and wage assistance* are used interchangeably throughout the report. By definition, they include all cases receiving either relief or having one or more members employed on the Works Program.

and over) increased in importance. The relative importance of
the youngest age group (under 16) varied more from month to month
but showed no significant tendency to permanent increase or
decrease during the year (fig. 2 and appendix table 8). The
probable explanation is that persons in all the age groups except
the youngest (under 16) were capable of independent movement on
and off relief. Children (under 16), however, necessarily moved
on and off relief only as part of families whose other members
were in age groups over 16 years. It would appear, therefore,
that over a period of time changes in the age distribution of
the relief population are least likely to occur in the age group
under 16 years.

Trend by Sex

The relative declines in the number of men and women receiving
relief or wage assistance were the same: each fell 11 percent.
The declines in the age groups under 45 years, for each sex, were
greater than the decline in the 45—64 group. In the oldest age
group, 65 years and over, the number of men receiving relief or
wage assistance rose nearly 2 percent during the year, while
the number of women fell more than 2 percent (appendix table 7).

Trend by Race

The decline in the number of Negroes receiving aid was less
than that of white persons.[9] This was true within each age
group except the group 65 and over.[10] For each race the three
younger age groups (under 16, 16—24, and 25—44 years) fell
more than the older age groups (appendix table 9).

Trend of Relief and Wage Assistance to Cases

Trend by Size of Case

The average size of case declined very little during the year
(appendix table 10). The relief and wage assistance load of
family cases, following an insignificant rise from December 1934
to January 1935, declined steadily to July, at which time it
was 8 percent below that of December 1934; at the end of the
year it was still 5 percent below. There was a substantial drop
in the number of cases with three or more persons. On the other
hand, the nonfamily (or one-person) case load, after a decline
during the summer months, rose during the balance of the year
and by December 1935 was 8 percent above the level of December

---

[9]Races other than white and Negro, comprising less than 2 percent of the
persons receiving relief or wage assistance in the 13 cities, have been
excluded from the race comparisons.

[10]In June 1935 many unemployable cases in Atlanta were closed by transfer
from the emergency relief administration to the department of public welfare.
This caused many persons 65 years of age and over to leave the relief rolls.
Exhaustion of funds of the local emergency relief administration in November resulted in additional separations of aged persons from relief.

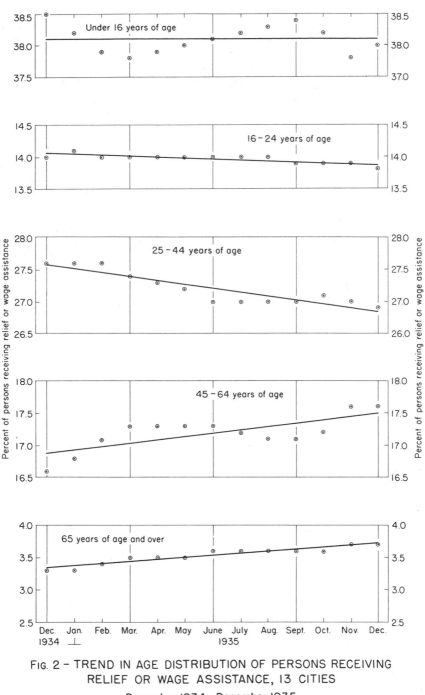

FIG. 2 – TREND IN AGE DISTRIBUTION OF PERSONS RECEIVING
RELIEF OR WAGE ASSISTANCE, 13 CITIES

December 1934 – December 1935

Source: Table 8.

AF-3003, WPA

1934 (fig. 3 and appendix table 11). An increase in the total number of persons in one- and two-person cases was more than offset by the decline in the total number in cases of three persons or more. These factors caused the number of persons receiving relief or wage assistance to decline relatively more than the number of cases.

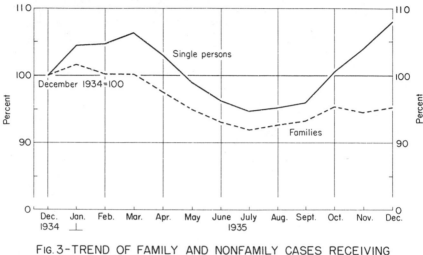

FIG. 3 - TREND OF FAMILY AND NONFAMILY CASES RECEIVING RELIEF OR WAGE ASSISTANCE, 13 CITIES

December 1934 – December 1935

Source: Table 11   AF–3004, WPA

Trend of Relief and Wage Assistance to Cases With Workers and Cases Without Workers

About nine-tenths of the cases had one or more workers in the case.[11] These cases declined 7 percent during the year, while the number of cases without workers showed little change, declining less than 1 percent (appendix table 12).

Trend of Relief and Wage Assistance to Workers

Trend by Sex

About 70 percent of all workers were men, and about 30 percent were women. The number of male workers receiving aid declined 9 percent during the year, while the number of female workers declined 7 percent. The distribution of workers by sex at the end of 1935 showed little change from that at the beginning of the year (appendix table 13).

---

[11]Workers are defined as persons between the ages of 16 and 64 years who are working or seeking work.

Trend by Race

During the year the number of white workers receiving relief or wage assistance declined 9 percent and the number of Negro workers declined 7 percent. In both December 1934 and December 1935 the relative proportions of each group in the total worker load remained practically the same: in both months white workers constituted about three-fourths and Negro workers about one-fourth of all workers receiving aid (appendix table 13).

Trend by Experience Status

Approximately nine-tenths of the cases had one or more workers 16—64 years of age who were either working or seeking work. In every 100 of these cases there were about 145 workers, of whom 22 were without previous work experience.[12]

Between December 1934 and December 1935 the number of inexperienced workers receiving aid declined 8.3 percent. Experienced workers showed close to the same proportionate decline (appendix table 13).

Trend by Socio-Economic Groups of Experienced Workers

Of all experienced workers receiving aid in December 1934, about a third were unskilled workers, another third were semiskilled workers, a sixth were skilled, and the remaining sixth were white-collar workers. Each of these four major occupational groups receiving aid declined during the year but in different proportions. Skilled workers showed the greatest net decline (15.7 percent); then followed semiskilled workers (10.3 percent), unskilled workers (7.2 percent), and white-collar workers (1.5 percent) (appendix table 14).

Approximately two-thirds of the white-collar workers were former clerks. The remaining third had been proprietors and professional workers. During the year the number of clerks and professional workers receiving aid declined while the number of proprietors increased. Unskilled workers receiving aid were about equally divided between laborers and domestic and personal service workers. Each of these groups declined during the year.

During the year there was an increase in the relative importance of the white-collar group and a decrease in that of the skilled group. In the semiskilled and unskilled groups the marked seasonal changes make it difficult to make any statement concerning trends (fig. 4 and appendix table 15).

---

[12]In this study an inexperienced worker is defined as one who has not worked on a job for at least 1 day a week for 4 consecutive weeks sometime during the 10-year period prior to interview.

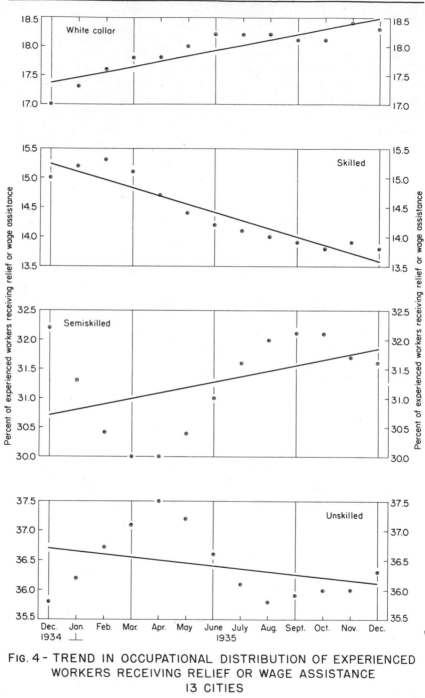

FIG. 4 - TREND IN OCCUPATIONAL DISTRIBUTION OF EXPERIENCED
WORKERS RECEIVING RELIEF OR WAGE ASSISTANCE
13 CITIES
December 1934 - December 1935

Source: Table 15.

AF-3005, WPA

Trend by Usual Industry of Experienced Workers

Wider variations occurred in the trends of industrial groups[13] receiving aid than of occupational groups. The greatest variation in the occupational groups occurred between skilled workers and white-collar workers, where the spread between percentage declines was approximately 14 percent (appendix table 14). However, among the industrial groups the number of workers on relief that were usually employed in the automobile industry declined 49 percent during 1935 while the number in the food group increased 15 percent, making a spread of 64 percent between the two industrial groups (appendix table 16).

The basis for this greater variation in trend between industrial groups receiving aid than between occupational groups is found in the fact that during periods of business expansion improvement in the various industries is by no means uniform. Indeed, retrenchment frequently takes place in some industries, while large gains are being made in others. Generally speaking, adverse trends in a given industry cause workers from each of the major occupational groups to be laid off. At the same time, expansion in another industry results in separations from the relief rolls of workers in each of the major occupational groups. Thus, for a given occupational group favorable developments in one industry tend to offset less favorable or unfavorable developments in another. This offsetting tendency causes the occupational groups to show less fluctuation than the industrial groups receiving aid.

Despite the differences in fluctuations of the various industrial groups during the year, the importance of each group among the workers on relief did not change markedly between December 1934 and December 1935. Workers in the automobile industry showed the greatest change.

Trend of Employment by Industrial Groups and Numbers Receiving Aid

Evidence of the close relationship between employment and relief is found in a comparison of the number of workers receiving aid with the volume of employment, by industrial groups. Since employment data are not available for the 13 cities, employment estimates for the entire United States have been used. A comparison of relief and wage assistance loads in the 13 cities with estimated employment in the United States is subject to

---

[13]The present discussion is limited for the most part to seven industrial groups—building and construction, iron and steel, automobile factories and repair shops, food and allied industries, transportation and communication, retail and wholesale trade, and domestic and personal service. These 7 groups comprised three-fourths of all the experienced workers on relief in the 13 cities in December 1934; each of these groups contained 4 percent or more of the 13-city relief load at that time.

many limitations.[14] Nevertheless, it is believed that such a comparison is sufficiently reliable to indicate the influence of employment changes upon relief and wage assistance trends.

Among the industrial groups there was a marked tendency for the number of workers receiving aid to decrease as employment increased and vice versa.[15] This relationship between employment and the number receiving aid was especially striking in three of the seven industrial groups—automobiles, iron and steel, and building and construction. It was least evident in the food and trade groups.[16] In the food group, however, it should be pointed out that activity in the canning industry, which is inadequately represented in the 13 cities, caused a marked rise in the employment index during the early fall. This rise had no counterpart in the 13-city relief load (fig. 5 and appendix table 17).

---

[14]First, the various industrial groups are not uniformly represented in the 13 cities; the degree of coverage ranges from 33.0 percent of urban United States in the case of automobile factories and repair shops to 5.9 percent in the case of mineral extraction. Second, for some of the industrial groups conditions in the 13 cities in 1935 were not fair measures of conditions throughout the country. For example, the textile industry suffered relatively more in the 13 cities than in the country at large. Third, the data serving as the basis for some of the employment estimates are known to be inadequate. Fourth, it should be noted that the number on relief in December 1934, the month used as the base for all relief-load trends, is an estimate in every instance and hence is subject to some margin of error. This means that percentage variations above or below December 1934 may be overstated or understated. However, the direction of the change—whether an increase or a decrease—is correctly shown.

[15]In comparing the trend of employable persons on relief with the trend of employment, it is important to note that a person who receives last relief at any time within a given month is not removed from the load until the following month. Thus, a person who secures a job on March 10 and receives his last relief grant the next day is included in the case-load figures for March but is not considered a part of the April case load unless he receives further relief in April. Having begun work by the middle of March, however, he is included in the March employment estimate. His job is first reflected in the employment estimate for March, but his separation from the relief rolls does not affect the load until April. For this reason case-load figures for one month should be compared, not with employment estimates for the same month but with estimates for the preceding month. It is also true that some cases coming on relief lost their private employment and received a relief grant in the same calendar month. The number of such cases, however, was comparatively small. The 1935 data indicate that at the time of admission to relief only 24 percent of the workers in accessions were unemployed less than 1 month, and the median average duration of unemployment was about 3 months. Consequently, the relationship between loss of job and accession to relief is apt to be spread over several months. In fig. 5 employment data are moved forward 1 month in all instances. November 1934 is taken as 100 percent for all employment series; December 1934, for all series of relief loads. December 1934 employment is plotted opposite the January 1935 relief load; January employment, opposite the February relief load; and so on.

[16]The 8 industrial groups receiving aid which are discussed here—building and construction, iron and steel, automobiles, transportation and communication, food, trade, domestic and personal service, and miscellaneous—include all experienced workers in the relief population of the 13 cities. Some of the employment estimates are those by Nathan, Robert R. in "Estimates of Unemployment in the United States, 1929—1935," *International Labour Review*, Vol. 33, No. 1, January 1936, extended through 1935; the others have been computed by using a method similar to that used by Mr. Nathan.

ACCESSION AND SEPARATION RATES OF PERSONS, CASES, AND WORKERS
ON THE RELIEF ROLLS OF 13 CITIES DURING 1935

A comparison of the number of persons or cases receiving relief or wage assistance between December 1934 and December 1935 shows the change in the size of the relief load between the beginning and end of the year, but it does not show the extent of the month-to-month movement on and off relief. Moreover, the net change in the relief rolls as shown by the number under care in December 1934 and December 1935 understates the amount of change that went on within the relief population during the year. Thus, if 1,000 cases are added to the relief rolls in a given month and 2,000 are removed, the net effect upon the load is the same as though the accessions and separations were 11,000 and 12,000, respectively, or any other numbers differing by a like amount.

Between the beginning and end of the year the number of cases receiving relief or wage assistance in the survey cities declined on an average of one-half of 1 percent a month. During this same period, however, the average monthly separation rate approximated $5\frac{1}{2}$ percent of the case load while the average accession rate approximated 5 percent a month.[17] Thus, the accession rate and the separation rate were each about 10 times as large as the net change in the relief case load.

Accessions to the relief rolls consist of new cases—i.e., cases new to relief in a given city—and of reopened cases—i.e., cases which have been on relief at least once before. More than two-fifths of the total accessions were cases that had never received relief in their respective cities. Approximately a sixth of these had a prior relief history in some other city. Therefore, if the proportion of new cases (44 percent) in accessions is reduced by a sixth to account for those new cases that had received relief at some time in another city, it is apparent that somewhat more than a third of all cases admitted to relief in the survey cities during the year had received no previous relief. During the course of the year the proportion of new cases in total accessions decreased slightly (appendix table 18).

---

[17]Accession and separation rates are computed by expressing the volume of accessions and of separations as percentages of the total number of cases receiving relief some time during the month. Since a case is considered closed in the month following that in which last relief was received, the separations of a given month may be regarded as applicable to the preceding month's load. Similarly, the accessions of a given month may also be thought of as applicable to the load of the preceding month. For this reason, in computing the separation and accession rates for a given month, the number of cases receiving relief some time during the preceding month has been used as the base. Computed in this way, a given month's accession rate minus its separation rate is the percent change in the load from the preceding month. Separation rates used throughout this report include all separations from the relief rolls except those for Works Program employment. Works Program closings have not been included because they are in the nature of a transfer of the relief load from one agency to another.

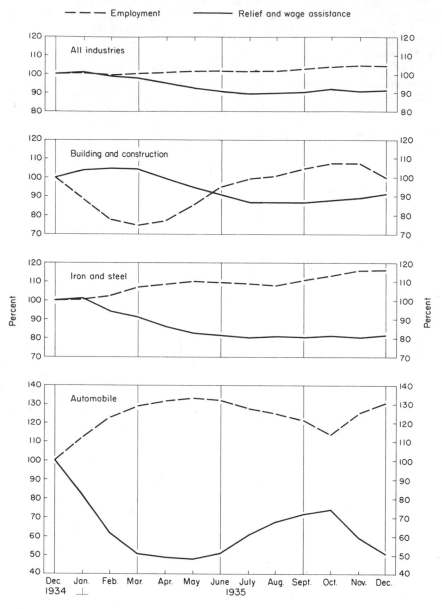

FIG. 5 – TREND OF EMPLOYMENT IN THE UNITED STATES AND OF
EXPERIENCED WORKERS RECEIVING RELIEF OR WAGE
ASSISTANCE, BY USUAL INDUSTRIAL GROUPS
13 CITIES

December 1934 — December 1935

Note: For employment, November 1934 = 100 %;
for relief and wage assistance, December 1934 = 100 %.
All employment data moved forward 1 month.

AF–3006, WPA

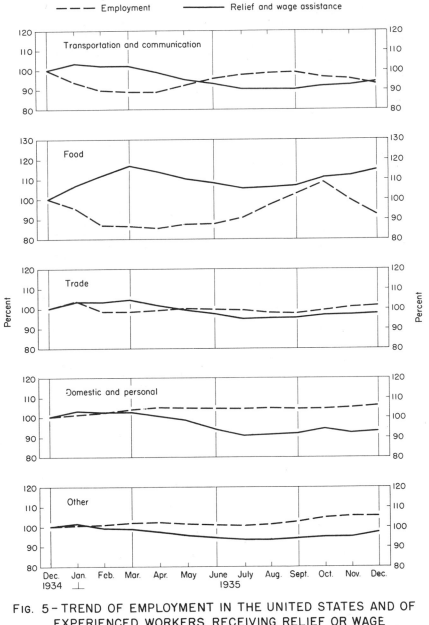

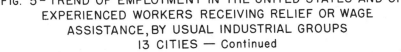

FIG. 5 – TREND OF EMPLOYMENT IN THE UNITED STATES AND OF
EXPERIENCED WORKERS RECEIVING RELIEF OR WAGE
ASSISTANCE, BY USUAL INDUSTRIAL GROUPS
13 CITIES — Continued

December 1934 — December 1935

Note: For employment, November 1934 = 100 % ;
for relief and wage assistance, December 1934 = 100 %.
All employment data moved forward 1 month.

AF-3013, WPA

This group of new cases with no prior relief comprised about 6,700 cases a month in the 13 cities. The total relief population of these cities was approximately a tenth of the relief population of urban United States. A rough estimate, therefore, indicates that about 67,000 new cases were added each month during 1935 to urban relief rolls in the United States; this occurred despite the fact that 1935 was, on the whole, a year of economic recovery.

The turnover of persons and workers in the relief population was quite similar to that of cases. The turnover of persons was slightly less than that of cases because of the comparatively low accession and separation rates for large families (appendix table 19).

Accession and Separation Rates for Persons

Accession and Separation Rates by Age Groups

The average monthly accession rate for all persons on relief during the year was 4.3 percent; the separation rate was 5.3 percent. Of the different age groups persons 25—44 years old showed the highest turnover; the most employable group of workers in the relief population is to be found in this age group. The turnover of persons in the age group 65 years and over was considerably below the general average; the accession and separation rates approximated four-fifths and three-fifths, respectively, of those for the group 25—44 years of age (appendix table 20).

Accession and Separation Rates by Sex

The movement on and off relief of men 25—44 years of age was a fourth higher than that of women in this age group. The average monthly turnover, however, was only a tenth greater for all men than for all women. The turnover for men was highest in the group 25—44 years, while that for women was highest in the age group 16—24 years (appendix table 20).

Accession and Separation Rates by Race

Average monthly turnover of Negro persons on relief was considerably smaller than that of white persons. This was true of all age groups and of both sexes. The average monthly accession rate for Negroes was 2.7 percent as compared with 4.9 percent for whites. Average monthly separation rates were 3.4 percent for Negroes and 6.0 percent for whites. For both whites and Negroes maximum turnover occurred in the age group 25—44. Minimum turnover occurred in the youngest and the oldest age groups (appendix table 20).

Accession and Separation Rates of Cases

Accession and Separation Rates by Size of Case

In general, the larger the case, the lower was the turnover. Accession and separation rates of one-person cases considerably exceeded the rates of other case sizes. Outside of the one-person cases differences in the rates by case size were less pronounced (appendix table 21).

Accession and Separation Rates of Cases With Workers and Cases Without Workers

Notwithstanding the absence of workers, monthly separation rates of cases without workers were approximately two-thirds those of cases with workers. Cases without workers had an average monthly accession rate of 3.8 percent; those with workers, 5.2 percent. The average monthly separation rate of cases without workers was 3.9 percent; of cases with workers, 5.8 percent.[18]

Accession and Separation Rates of Workers

Accession and Separation Rates by Race and Sex

The turnover of Negro workers was approximately two-thirds that of white workers. Accession and separation rates for female workers of all races combined approximated four-fifths those for male workers. By sex and race, accession and separation rates were definitely lower for male and female Negro workers than corresponding rates for white workers (appendix table 22).

Accession and Separation Rates by Experience Status.

Turnover of inexperienced workers approximated three-fourths that of experienced workers. The average monthly accession rate of inexperienced workers was 3.5 percent; that of experienced workers, 5.1 percent. The average monthly separation rate of inexperienced workers was 4.3 percent; that of experienced workers, 5.9 percent. Only a small part of the separations from relief of inexperienced workers can be attributed to their own private employment; most of these workers were young persons who left the relief rolls because some experienced worker in the case was able to secure employment.

Accession and Separation Rates by Socio-Economic Groups of Experienced Workers

Among experienced workers average monthly accession and separation rates were highest for skilled and semiskilled workers and lowest for white-collar and unskilled workers. In the white-collar subgroups turnover was lowest in the clerical group.

---

[18]From unpublished data in the files of the Division of Research.

Among unskilled workers accession and separation rates of domestic and personal service workers were considerably below
those of manual laborers (appendix table 23).

*Accession and Separation Rates by Usual Industry of Experienced
Workers*

Average monthly relief accession and separation rates of
experienced workers from the automobile industry were higher in
1935 than those of any other industrial group. The separation
rate of this group was almost double the accession rate. Improvement in the iron and steel industry also caused the separation rate of that industrial group to exceed the accession
rate by a wide margin. Adverse employment trends in the food
industry, on the other hand, made the accession rate of this
group higher than the separation rate (appendix tables 24 and
25).

Seasonal changes of employment in the various industries were
reflected in monthly fluctuations of accession and separation
rates. Thus, among building workers relief accession rates were
highest during the winter and fall and separation rates were
highest during the spring and summer. In the automobile group
relief accession rates were highest during the summer slack;
separation rates were highest in the fall and winter busy season.

REASONS FOR OPENING AND CLOSING RELIEF CASES IN 13 CITIES DURING 1935

The majority of the relief case accessions and separations
in the survey cities during 1935 were caused by loss or gain
of private employment. During the last 10 months of the year
slightly more than a half of total accessions were caused by
loss of job less than 4 months prior to receipt of the first
relief grant; 6.5 percent were caused by decreased hours of work
or rate of pay; and 14.1 percent were caused by loss or depletion
of resources (appendix tables 26, 27, and 28).

Corresponding reasons for removing cases from the relief rolls
include employment secured in private industry and increased
hours of work or rate of pay. These reasons were responsible
for 50.8 percent and 7.0 percent, respectively, of total regular
closings[19] (appendix table 29). In addition, a substantial
number of the cases were closed because of failure to report to
the agency granting relief; many of these cases actually had
members in private employment at the time the case was closed.[20]
This nonreporting group represents about a seventh of the separations throughout a 10-month period. When some allowance is

---

[19]Regular closings include all relief closings except those for Works
Program employment.

[20]See p. 19.

made for this fact, it appears that between 60 and 70 percent of all accessions and separations were caused by changes in employment status.

Available data for the last 5 months of the year indicate that loss of aid from friends and relatives ranked next in importance to changes in employment status as a reason for opening cases, accounting for about a sixth of total accessions. Administrative policy, discharges from institutions, transfers from other public and private relief agencies, and miscellaneous other reasons accounted for less than a tenth of the openings.

Receipt of aid from friends and relatives ranked second in importance to employment in private industry as a reason for closing relief cases. Income from sources outside the case, such as discovery of unrealized assets and financial aid, ranked third.

Reasons for Opening and Closing Family and Nonfamily Relief Cases

Loss of employment, which was the principal factor responsible for the opening of both family and nonfamily cases during the last 10 months of the year, was more important for family than for nonfamily cases. The three reasons directly related to employment—loss of private employment within 4 months, decreased hours of work or rate of pay, and loss or depletion of resources—accounted for an average of 82 percent of the family and 63 percent of the nonfamily openings.

Family cases applied for relief sooner after loss of private employment than did nonfamily cases. Loss of job within 4 months was a more important reason for the accession of family than of nonfamily cases. On the other hand, loss or depletion of resources and loss of aid from friends and relatives accounted for greater proportions of total openings for nonfamily than for family cases (figs. 0 and 7 and appendix tables 30 and 31).

Comparison of the reasons for closing family and nonfamily cases is difficult because of a large client-failed-to-report category in the nonfamily group. For family cases employment in private industry combined with increased hours of work or pay accounted for nearly three-fourths of all separations during the last 10 months of the year. The corresponding proportion for nonfamily cases was only one-fourth. However, it is not improbable that many of the separations in the client-failed-to-report category were caused by private employment.[21] While

---

[21]Two facts may be cited as evidence that the client-failed-to-report category contains a considerable number of private-employment closings. In the first place, more than 70 percent of the nonfamily closed cases are males between the ages 25—64 years, inclusive, divided about equally between those under and those over 44 years of age. Nonfamily persons—largely able-bodied men with few or no dependents—are able to move about freely in search of employment opportunities and to accept employment away from their homes. In the second place, because of lesser mobility and greater continuous need of assistance, family cases tend to maintain closer contact with the relief agency than do nonfamily cases and hence are more apt to report their employment status.

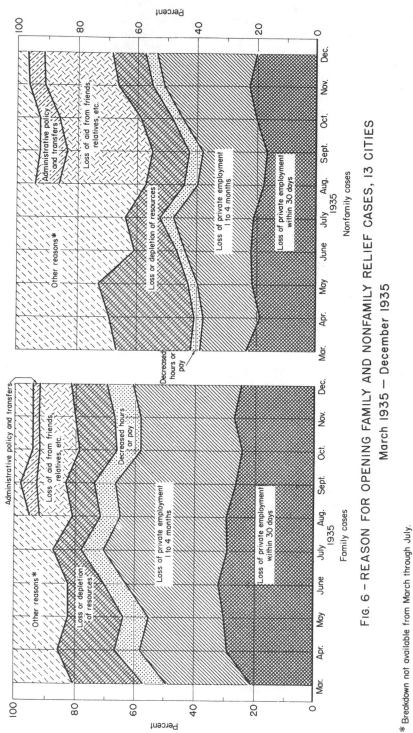

FIG. 6 – REASON FOR OPENING FAMILY AND NONFAMILY RELIEF CASES, 13 CITIES

March 1935 – December 1935

* Breakdown not available from March through July.

Source: Table 30.

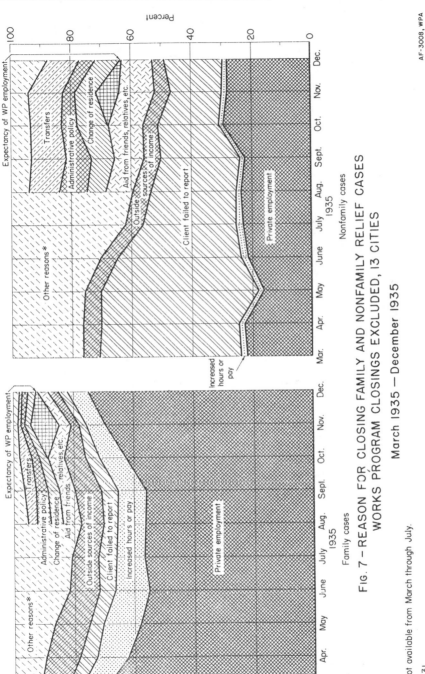

FIG. 7 — REASON FOR CLOSING FAMILY AND NONFAMILY RELIEF CASES
WORKS PROGRAM CLOSINGS EXCLUDED, 13 CITIES

March 1935 — December 1935

* Breakdown not available from March through July.

Source: Table 31.

AF-3008, WPA

this category (client-failed-to-report) accounted for only 5 percent of all family case separations, it accounted for 34 percent of the nonfamily case separations.

A detailed analysis of reasons for separation not directly associated with employment is available only for the last 5 months of the year. The proportion of nonfamily cases closed for reasons not directly associated with employment status was at least twice that of family cases.

Reasons for Opening and Closing White and Negro Relief Cases

Loss or decrease of employment—the principal reason for opening cases—accounted for over three-fourths of the accessions of white cases but less than two-thirds of the Negro cases. On the other hand, loss of aid from friends and relatives was responsible for only about a seventh of all white cases but over a fourth of all Negro cases admitted to relief during the last 5 months of the year[22] (appendix tables 26, 27, and 28).

Among relief cases closed, the percentage of separations from relief because of jobs secured in private industry and increased hours or pay was a third higher for white cases than for Negro cases, but receipt of aid from friends and relatives caused less than half as many closings among whites as among Negroes[23] (appendix table 29).

Reasons for Closing Cases Without Workers

Data pertaining to reasons for closing cases without workers were obtained only for May and October 1935. More than three-fifths of these closings in both months were due to aid from friends and relatives, outside sources of income, transfers to other agencies and institutions, and death. A small proportion of the closings—about a sixteenth in both months—was attributable to private employment.[24] Between these months there was

---

[22]Detailed tabulations of "other reasons" were made only for the last 5 months of 1935.

[23]Another racial difference is to be found in the closing of relief cases because of "expectancy of Works Program employment." While this reason accounted for less than 1 percent of the white cases closed, it accounted for 12 percent of the Negro cases closed. Examination of individual city data shows that only one city—Atlanta—reported this item among the reasons for closing; it occurred for the most part in November when, on the 15th, the emergency relief administration in Atlanta closed its doors because of complete exhaustion of funds. Subsequent to November 15 relief was administered in Atlanta by the Fulton County Department of Public Welfare. Because of shortage of funds, many Atlanta cases on the active relief rolls in October received no relief in November. According to the definition of a closing, it was necessary to regard such cases as closed in November, unless they had already been closed because of Works Program employment. In a number of instances efforts to place them on the Program had failed up to November 30 and expectancy of Works Program employment was assigned as the reason for closing.

[24]Workers are defined as persons between the ages 16 and 64 years who are working or seeking work. In a few instances persons outside the age group 16—64 years were able to secure Works Program employment or sufficient private employment to close their cases.

a sharp drop in outside sources of income as a reason for closing and a large increase in transfers to agencies or institutions.

In both months outside sources of income and private employment were considerably more important as reasons for closing white cases without workers than Negro cases. On the other hand, the proportion of closings because of aid from relatives and friends and death was larger for Negro than for white cases (appendix table 32).

OCCUPATIONAL AND INDUSTRIAL SHIFTS OF EXPERIENCED WORKERS EMPLOYED AT TIME OF CLOSING IN 13 CITIES DURING 1935

Inexperienced Workers With Jobs at Closing

Inexperienced workers comprised less than an eighth of all workers in regular closings[25] during the last 6 months of the year (appendix table 33). Of this one-eighth only a very small proportion had private jobs at time of closing. On the other hand, about three-fifths of the experienced workers in regular closings had private employment. Because of the very small number of employed inexperienced workers, the discussion of occupational and industrial shifts which follows is limited to experienced workers employed at the time their relief cases were closed.

Occupational Shifts

Regardless of their usual occupations, many workers on relief took whatever nonrelief jobs there were available. Data obtained for the last 6 months of the year indicate the extent to which experienced workers from the relief rolls secured private employment at their usual occupational levels. There were insufficient jobs to absorb all the employed white-collar, skilled, and semiskilled groups at their usual occupations. About a fifth of these workers had to accept jobs outside their usual occupational employment. For example, skilled workers made up 17.5 percent of all those employed at closing, but only 14.8 percent of all jobs held were in the skilled category. This suggests that opportunities to shift into skilled jobs were small and that skilled workers succeeded in obtaining work at other occupations. What has been said of the skilled worker also applies to the white-collar and semiskilled but to a much lesser extent. As a result of this crowding by other groups, the unskilled worker found himself at a disadvantage in competing for jobs in private industry (appendix table 34).

The displacement of unskilled workers by those in more skilled groups was limited largely to white workers. Most of the crowding of the unskilled group came from the white-collar and skilled

---

[25] By definition a regular closing is any relief case closing except one having Works Program employment.

groups. Among Negroes these two latter groups constituted only about a tenth of the total employed at time of closing. Among whites, however, the white-collar and skilled workers accounted for over a third of all workers employed at closing.

The greatest proportionate shift occurred out of the skilled workers' group. About three-tenths of all workers employed at closing whose usual occupations were in the skilled category held jobs outside the skilled group. The corresponding shifts out of other groups were only slightly less for white-collar workers: the shift was about a fifth for semiskilled workers and only about an eighth for unskilled workers (appendix table 35).

About a third of those who shifted moved upward, and the remaining two-thirds moved downward.[26] About a sixth of the skilled workers who shifted moved upward into the white-collar group. The remainder that shifted downward were about equally divided between semiskilled and unskilled jobs. Among those usually employed at white-collar occupations, about a seventh of those who shifted went into skilled work; the remainder held semiskilled and unskilled jobs in about equal proportions. Of the semiskilled workers who shifted, approximately three-fifths moved downward into the unskilled group, while those who moved upward were divided about equally between white-collar and skilled work. The majority of unskilled workers who shifted upward were absorbed in the semiskilled group.

The proportionate shift out of each occupational group was greater for Negroes than for whites, except in the unskilled category. Also, as might be expected, the proportionate downward shift of white-collar, skilled, and semiskilled workers was much greater for Negroes than for whites. Likewise, the upward shift of Negroes was smaller than that for whites.

Industrial Shifts

The usual industry of employed workers in closed cases was about the same as that of workers in the relief population as a whole. Moreover, the jobs held at the time of closing were distributed among the various industries in about the same proportion as workers in the relief load. To illustrate, 5.9 percent of the workers receiving relief during the months June through September 1935 reported iron and steel as the industry of usual employment; 5.9 percent of the workers who were employed at the time their cases were closed usually worked in the iron and steel group; and 6.0 percent reported having jobs in the iron and steel industry. The widest differences occurred in

---

[26]In this report occupational groups are ranked in the following order: white-collar, skilled, semiskilled, and unskilled. Movement in the direction of the unskilled group is termed *a downward shift*. Conversely, movement in the direction of the white-collar group is termed *an upward shift*.

the automobile, domestic and personal service, and miscellaneous groups (appendix table 36).

Among the major industrial groups slightly more than a fourth of the workers shifted to jobs outside the industry of their usual employment. At the one extreme, nearly two-fifths of the group usually employed in transportation and communication shifted to other industries. At the other extreme, only about a seventh of the workers usually employed in the domestic and personal service group moved to other industries (appendix tables 37 and 38). No attempt has been made to measure the shift from one kind of work to another within a given industry.

Negroes evidently encountered greater difficulty than whites in finding work outside the industry in which they had usually been employed. Among employed white workers over a fourth were outside their usual industry; the corresponding proportion for Negroes was only about a fifth (appendix table 37).

SUPPLEMENTATION OF PRIVATE-EMPLOYMENT EARNINGS WITH RELIEF IN 13 CITIES DURING 1935

In addition to the cases which were wholly dependent upon direct relief in 1935, there were cases in which one or more workers were employed part time or full time in private industry. Their earnings were so low, however, that it was necessary to grant relief to these cases.

Proportion of Relief Cases Having Private-Employment Earnings

Less than a seventh of the cases on relief throughout May 1935 received nonrelief earnings. Among cases coming on relief in 1935, the proportion having private-employment income during the month of admission to relief declined in importance during the year (appendix table 39). Supplementation was more prevalent in reopened and large cases than in new and small cases. Since reopened cases were larger than new cases, the difference in supplementation of new and reopened cases amounted largely to a case-size difference. Supplementation was more common in Negro cases than in white cases, which cannot be explained by the size of the case but rather by the more extensive part-time employment among Negroes than among whites (appendix table 39).

Differences in supplementation among small and large cases are also available for 12 of the 13 survey cities in May 1934.[27] The May 1935 proportion of cases with private employment was smaller for each case size than the May 1934 proportion (appendix table 40). A part of this decline was doubtless caused by

---

[27] May 1934 data for 12 of the 13 survey cities was obtained from unpublished source tables of the published study by Palmer, Gladys L. and Wood, Katherine D., *Urban Workers on Relief,* Part I—The Occupational Characteristics of Workers on Relief in Urban Areas May 1934, Research Monograph IV, Division of Social Research, Works Progress Administration, Washington, D. C., 1936. Omaha was not included in this study.

an FERA ruling, issued on September 18, 1934, against supplementing the full-time earnings of workers employed in private industry. However, a difference between the 1934 and the 1935 data should be noted: A small number of closed cases are included in the May 1934 study, perhaps causing a slight overstatement of the extent of supplementation, whereas the May 1935 study is limited to cases on relief throughout the month.

Income of Supplemented and Nonsupplemented Relief Cases

The average relief benefit to supplemented cases on relief throughout the month of May 1935 was about three-fourths that of nonsupplemented cases (appendix table 41). Private-employment income in these cases was almost as large as the average relief benefit, but one-third of these private earnings was offset by reduced relief. The combined nonrelief earnings and relief income of supplemented cases averaged one and a half times the relief income of nonsupplemented cases, so that two-thirds of the private earnings accrued to the case as additional income (appendix tables 42 and 43).

It may be questioned why relief benefits were not reduced by the total of the income from private employment. This was not done for several reasons. First, because of the job there were outlays for lunches, transportation, and clothing which made increased allowances necessary for these budget items. Second, there were many instances in which the employed workers were the older children in their respective families, and in order to keep them from leaving home, they were often allowed to retain a considerable portion of their earnings for personal use. Third, unless the worker on relief received some monetary benefit as a result of the job, he might have been discouraged from taking it.

Characteristics of Workers in Supplemented Cases

Employed Workers in Cases Admitted to Relief by Sex and Race[28]

The proportion of women having private employment was about twice that of men in both white and Negro cases coming on relief. The proportion of all Negroes having private employment was somewhat greater than the proportion of all whites, which may be accounted for by the preponderance of servants among Negro women and the low earnings through part-time employment of the servant group (appendix table 44).

---

[28]Some persons were considered employed when admitted to relief, though they were not actually working. For the most part, these persons were temporarily idle as a result of strikes or illness. They constituted approximately 1 percent of the experienced employable persons in the 1935 relief accessions in the 13 cities.

Occupational Distribution of Jobs Held[29]

One-fifth of all workers employed while on relief in May 1934 in 12 of the survey cities held white-collar jobs; almost one-third held semiskilled jobs; more than one-third were engaged in unskilled work; and only one-eighth were in skilled work. Servants alone, in the unskilled group, accounted for almost one-fourth of the total workers in all supplemented cases in May 1934. Occupational distributions of jobs held by persons admitted to relief in 1935 in all of the survey cities and of employed persons in the May 1934 load in 12 of these cities are shown in appendix table 45.

The occupational distribution for employed whites was about the same as that for all workers employed at time of admission to relief. But for employed Negroes coming on relief, jobs were heavily concentrated in the unskilled category: two-thirds were engaged in unskilled work; and the servant classification alone accounted for one-half of the jobs held by this group.

Industrial Distribution of Jobs Held

About one-fourth of all workers employed while on relief in May 1934, in 12 of the survey cities, were in domestic and personal service; almost one-fifth were in trade; and one-fourth were in 5 industries combined—building and construction, iron and steel, automobile, transportation and communication, and food and allied industries. The other third were employed in miscellaneous industries. The industrial distributions of jobs held by persons admitted to relief in 1935 in the survey cities and by employed persons in the May 1934 relief load in 12 cities are shown in appendix table 46.

Wide differences exist between the industrial distributions of jobs held by whites and those held by Negroes at the time of admission to the relief rolls in 1935. More than a half of the Negroes were employed in domestic and personal service, while less than a fifth of the whites were employed in work of that kind.

UNEMPLOYMENT DURATION AND REEMPLOYMENT IN 13 CITIES DURING 1935

Reemployment opportunities for workers on relief varied with their experience, age, sex, race, occupational background, and duration of unemployment. The experienced workers on relief obtained self-supporting jobs during the latter part of 1935 at

---

[29]Data on jobs held by employed persons in the relief load are not available for 1935. However, May 1934 data are available for 12 of the 13 survey cities and for 79 cities and also for relief accessions in the 13 cities during 1935.

a rate four times that of inexperienced workers.[30] Among the experienced workers on relief reemployment rates were much higher for workers in the younger age groups than for workers in the older age groups; they were much higher for men than women, for whites than Negroes, and for skilled and semiskilled workers than for white-collar and unskilled workers.

Duration of unemployment had a greater bearing upon chances for reemployment than any other factor.[31] The reemployment rate of workers who had been unemployed less than 6 months was 12 times that of persons who had been out of work 2 years or more. Inasmuch as experienced workers unemployed 2 years or more constituted almost half of the experienced workers on relief, it is obvious that chances of reemployment were seriously restricted for a large number on the relief rolls.

Duration of Unemployment for Workers Upon Admission to Relief

About half of the experienced workers admitted to relief during 1935 in the survey cities had been unemployed less than 3 months; about a fourth had been unemployed for a year or more (appendix table 47); and workers in new relief cases, admitted between February and May 1935, had been unemployed for longer periods than those in reopened cases. Workers in new cases, because of greater resources, had been able to support themselves for longer periods after losing employment than had those in reopened cases.

Unemployment Duration by Age, Sex, and Race

Unemployment data relative to age, sex, and race of workers at time of admission to the relief rolls are available for February through May 1935. Resources upon which younger workers could draw were generally smaller than those of older people, and they consequently came on relief sooner after losing employment than did the older workers. The average duration of unemployment was higher for the age group 16—24 years than for any other group under 55 years. But for age groups above 24 years the average increased with age, beginning at 2.8 months for those 25—34 years and reaching 5.0 months for those 55—64 years (appendix table 48).

Women workers admitted to the relief rolls had been without work for much longer periods than had men. In only one age group (55—64) did the average unemployment period for men exceed that for women. A partial explanation is that women frequently

---

[30]Inexperienced workers are those who have not held a nonrelief job lasting 4 weeks or more during the last 10 years.

[31]Duration of unemployment has been computed from the time of last nonrelief job of 4 weeks or more. The period includes unemployment both before and after coming on relief. The data are necessarily limited to experienced workers.

did not seek employment until the head of the family lost his job. Consequently, they may have been without gainful work for long periods, although they had been seeking employment for only a short time.

Negroes and whites were unemployed about the same length of time. One would expect the period to have been shorter for whites, because of their greater resources, but an offsetting factor was that proportionately more Negroes than whites were supported by friends and relatives before coming on relief.

Unemployment Duration by Occupational Groups

The white-collar workers remained off relief for longer periods after loss of employment than did the skilled, semiskilled, or unskilled workers (appendix table 49). One might expect that unskilled workers would have the shortest period of unemployment prior to coming on relief, but their average period was actually longer than that for skilled and semiskilled workers, whose periods of unemployment averaged the same. Unskilled workers had better opportunities, however, than those in the other groups to secure employment at casual jobs—jobs lasting less than 4 weeks and therefore considered insufficient in this study to terminate the period of unemployment—and the income from these jobs tended to prolong the period of unemployment prior to acceptance of relief.

Duration of Unemployment for Workers at Time of Separation From Relief[32]

Workers leaving the relief rolls during the last 3 months of 1935 in regular closings had been unemployed on an average of about 8 months, while those in Works Program closings had been unemployed over three times as long. This would indicate that persons with short periods of unemployment were more readily reabsorbed into private employment than were persons with long periods of unemployment (fig. 8 and appendix tables 50 and 51).

Unemployment Duration by Age, Sex, and Race

Workers in the younger age groups, in both regular and Works Program closings, had been unemployed for much shorter periods, on the average, than had workers in the older age groups. However, the period of unemployment was much longer for workers in each age group in Works Program closings than for those in corresponding age groups in regular closings. The periods ranged from 12 months to 34 months for workers in Works Program closings and from 7 to 14 months for those in regular closings (appendix table 51).

In Works Program closings women had periods of unemployment somewhat shorter than those of men, but in regular closings

---

[32]Workers employed for at least 4 weeks prior to closing are not considered.

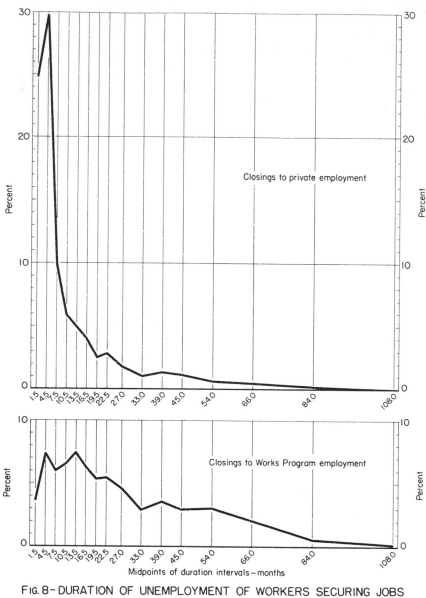

FIG. 8 – DURATION OF UNEMPLOYMENT OF WORKERS SECURING JOBS
AT CLOSING, REGULAR AND WORKS PROGRAM CLOSINGS
13 CITIES

October 1935 – December 1935

Note: For duration intervals exceeding 3 months,
the height of a given point has been obtained by reducing
the percent of workers in the given duration interval to a
3 months' average centering at the given point.
Presentation in this manner is necessary because of the
irregularity of the duration intervals in the data.

Source: Table 50.

AF-3009, WPA

their unemployment duration was more than double that of men. Workers of each sex in regular closings, though, had been on relief for a much shorter time than those in Works Program closings. The difference in unemployment duration between men and women, as pointed out in the discussion of accessions, is due in part to the fact that women frequently do not seek employment until the head of the family loses his job and that they had been without gainful employment for long periods prior to seeking work (appendix table 51).

Whites and Negroes in Works Program closings had both been unemployed, on an average, slightly over 2 years. In regular closings, however, the unemployment period for Negroes averaged more than twice that for whites, but for both races the median duration of unemployment was much lower than that for workers in Works Program closings (appendix table 52).

Unemployment Duration for Workers Securing Works Program Employment or Private Employment

About 55 percent of the experienced workers in regular closings secured jobs in private employment (appendix table 55). The average unemployment duration of the workers securing jobs was considerably less than that of all workers in these cases. Regular closings were heavily weighted with workers of comparatively short unemployment periods, and those with the shortest period had the best chances of reemployment. Comparisons by sex, race, and age groups also reveal marked differences (appendix table 53).

Slightly over a half of those who secured private jobs had been unemployed less than 6 months; only a ninth of the experienced workers assigned to Works Program jobs had been idle less than 6 months. Only about a seventh of those who obtained private employment had been without work 2 years or more, whereas approximately a half of the Works Program group had been idle for a like period (appendix table 54).

Although reemployment opportunities within a given group are best for those workers having a short unemployment period, caution must be exercised in drawing conclusions simply by comparing the unemployment duration of one group of workers with that of another group. Average duration of unemployment in some instances is not a valid measure of relative reemployment opportunities. In group comparisons it is possible for poor employment opportunities to be associated with short unemployment periods and good employment opportunities with long unemployment periods. For example, recent loss of jobs resulting in heavy relief accessions of one group of workers may cause the average duration of unemployment for that group to be relatively short. For another group good employment opportunities may result in few relief accessions and the removal from the relief rolls of large numbers of short-time unemployed. Under these conditions the average duration of unemployment for the group remaining on relief would be relatively long.

Separation Rates of Workers on Relief

Data on employment status at closing for workers leaving relief rolls are available for the 13 cities during the last 3 months of 1935. About 50 percent of all workers in regular closings secured private jobs at time of closing,[33] 11 percent were already privately employed while still on relief,[34] and 34 percent were unemployed. The employment status at closing was unknown for the remaining 5 percent (appendix table 55).

Separation Rates of Workers by Age, Sex, and Race

Workers in the younger age groups showed higher average monthly separation rates than those in the older groups, and those in the younger groups, above 16—19 years, found it easier to secure private employment than did older workers (appendix table 55).[35]

Male workers left the relief rolls at a higher rate than did female workers. Among those workers who left relief, more men than women were able to secure jobs at time of closing.

The separation rate was higher for white workers than for Negro workers, and jobs were more readily secured at time of closing by whites than by Negroes (appendix table 56).

Separation Rates of Inexperienced Workers

Inexperienced workers, approximating a seventh of the workers on relief, were largely young persons between 16 and 25 years of age. Men and women were about equal in number in this young group, but among those who were over 25 years women greatly outnumbered men (appendix table 58).

The separation rate of inexperienced workers was about three-fourths that of experienced workers and was highest for the group 16—19 years (appendix table 55). But some four-fifths of all inexperienced workers in closings left relief without jobs as against only one-fourth of the experienced workers. Some young workers were, of course, often taken off relief through the closing of cases by the employment of experienced workers.

---

[33] Includes all workers obtaining self-supporting private jobs during the last 4 weeks on relief. All but a small proportion of the workers reported as securing jobs obtained sufficient income to close their cases. Examination of the data shows that the number of employable persons securing jobs during the last 4 weeks on relief exceeded the number of employable cases closed because of private employment by approximately 3 percent.

[34] Workers employed at private jobs while still on relief for at least 4 weeks prior to closing.

[35] The monthly separation rate is the number of workers leaving the relief rolls for every 100 workers receiving relief. For a more complete statement see p. 13, footnote 17.

Separation Rates of Experienced Workers by Occupational Groups

During the last 3 months of 1935 the separation rates were highest for semiskilled workers and lowest for white-collar workers; in the other two groups the rate was higher for skilled workers than for unskilled. But the proportion of workers in closings who secured self-supporting private employment was highest for skilled workers (appendix table 57).

Separation Rates of Experienced Workers by Duration of Unemployment

Experienced workers unemployed for a short time had the best chance of leaving the relief rolls. Furthermore, the great bulk of workers leaving relief after short periods of idleness secured self-supporting jobs. But the majority of those who left relief after long periods of idleness did so for reasons other than their own private employment (appendix tables 59 and 60).

Reemployment Rates of Experienced Workers on Relief

Wide differences existed in reemployment rates by duration of unemployment.[36] Workers idle for only 3 to 4 months secured self-supporting jobs in private industry at a rate of about 14 percent a month. But reemployment opportunities decreased rapidly as the unemployment period increased, until workers idle 2 years or longer had very small chance of leaving relief through private employment (fig. 9 and appendix table 61). Since one-half of the workers on relief had been unemployed 2 years or more, the significance of this is apparent.

Reemployment Rates by Age, Sex, and Race

Reemployment rates were highest in the age group 25—34 years and decreased with each successive age group unemployed any specified length of time. The older groups had much larger proportions of long-time unemployed than did the younger groups and were therefore doubly handicapped in their search for reemployment (appendix tables 61 and 62).

A study of the May 1934 urban relief population revealed that women had been unemployed for shorter periods than men.[37] The

---

[36] By definition of a regular closing, the last month of relief is the month preceding that of closing. Consequently, October—December private-employment closings corresponded to jobs secured in September—November. The monthly reemployment rate is the number of experienced workers securing self-supporting private jobs at closing for every 100 unemployed experienced workers on relief.

[37] Palmer, Gladys L. and Wood, Katherine D., *Urban Workers on Relief*, Part I—The Occupational Characteristics of Workers on Relief in Urban Areas May 1934, Research Monograph IV, Division of Social Research, Works Progress Administration, Washington, D. C., 1936, p. 44.

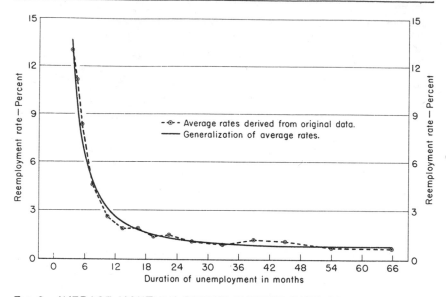

FIG. 9 – AVERAGE MONTHLY REEMPLOYMENT RATE OF EXPERIENCED
WORKERS ON RELIEF, BY DURATION OF UNEMPLOYMENT
13 CITIES

October 1935 — December 1935

Source: Table 61.   AF-3010, WPA

same situation prevailed for workers on relief in the 13 cities during the last 3 months of 1935. It was also discovered
that women workers on relief in the survey cities secured self-
supporting jobs at a rate only a third that of men (appendix
table 63). On the other hand, studies of workers in the general population have shown that displaced women found it easier
to obtain jobs than displaced men but suffered greater income
losses.[38] This difference may be due to the fact that the reemployment rate used in the present study was limited to relief
workers who secured jobs yielding enough income to close their
cases. Similar limitations were not imposed in connection with
the studies of the general population.

Negroes and whites on relief had been unemployed about the
same average periods. Half of each race were jobless 2 years
or more, but the rate at which whites—both males and females—
obtained self-supporting jobs at closing was more than double
that of Negroes. Irrespective of sex, white and Negro workers
with short unemployment periods had a much better chance of
reemployment than those who had been without work for comparatively long periods (appendix table 63).

---

[38] Weintraub, David and Posner, Harold L., *Unemployment and Increasing
Productivity*, National Research Project, Works Progress Administration,
Washington, D. C., 1937, p. 74.

Reemployment Rates by Occupational Groups

Workers in the four occupational groups differed considerably in their reemployment rates. Semiskilled workers were reemployed at a rate slightly above that of the skilled group and at a much greater rate than that of the unskilled and the white-collar groups (appendix table 64). This advantage for the semiskilled workers was caused largely by seasonal improvement in the automobile industry during the fall of 1935. Then, too, both semiskilled and skilled workers obtained work outside their occupational levels in greater numbers than did the unskilled and white-collar workers. This meant that they moved up or down in the occupational scale and filled jobs in the white-collar and unskilled levels. The disadvantage of the white-collar workers in reemployment opportunity may also be accounted for by the fact that even though they are discharged later in a depression, they are not rehired as soon as workers in the other groups. Within each occupational group, however, workers unemployed for a short time had the best chance of reemployment (appendix table 65).

THE ROLE OF THE WORKS PROGRAM

Relief grants under the Federal Emergency Relief Administration, created in 1933, were made on the basis of need. The amount of relief granted to a case was based upon its budgetary requirements and its income, if any, from outside sources. The difference between the budgetary requirements and the allowance made for outside income determined the amount of relief to be granted. Frequently, however, the actual relief grant fell below this amount because of a shortage of agency funds.

With the introduction of the Works Program in the latter part of 1935, the security wage[39] was substituted for the principle of budgetary deficiency. The security wage did not vary with the size of the case, as had the relief grant, but was predetermined to take account of the occupational classification of the job and the geographical area in which the work was done. It was, then, in the form of a monthly salary and was generally higher than the former relief grant; the majority of the relief cases transferred to the Works Program benefited substantially from the transfer.

The number of persons unemployed and the number of cases receiving relief or wage assistance, 1933—1936, are given in appendix table 66.

---

[39]The prevailing wage replaced the security wage on July 1, 1936 (Emergency Relief Administration Act of June 22, 1936, and WPA Administrative Order No. 41, June 22, 1936). In effect, the change amounted to retaining the monthly security payment but changing the hourly rate and the hours of work.

Cases Removed From the Relief Rolls in 13 Cities During 1935 by Works Program Employment

Relief cases closed because of Works Program employment up to December 31, 1935, in the survey cities were equal to about 44 percent of the July 1935 relief load (appendix table 67). Approximately two-thirds of these closings occurred during December.[40]

There was a sharp difference in representation of men and women on the Works Program. In terms of their respective relief populations, the proportion of women workers employed on the Program during 1935 was less than a fourth that of men. This was partly the result of difficulty encountered during the early months of the Program in providing suitable projects for women. Then, too, the head of the family, usually a man, was the one to be assigned to the Works Program.

Approximately equal proportions of the July 1935 relief load of Negro and white workers were employed on the Works Program. When, however, the proportions of the July load transferred to the Program are examined by sex, it is found that a much higher proportion of men than of women received assignment. Moreover, the proportion of Negro men was higher than the proportion of white men (appendix table 68). This was due to the large proportion of Negroes who were laborers, the largest occupational class on the Program.

The proportion of experienced workers on relief who obtained employment on the Works Program was over three times that of inexperienced workers. This resulted from the policy of assigning Works Program jobs to heads of cases who, as a rule, were experienced workers (appendix table 68).

Of the four major occupational groups—white-collar, skilled, semiskilled, and unskilled—assignments to the Works Program were relatively most numerous among the unskilled and least numerous among white-collar workers.

Comparison of Works Program Wage Rates With Relief Grants

Relief grants were based mainly upon need, and those for large families were necessarily much greater than those for small families (appendix table 69). But the monthly wage paid to a worker on the Works Program does not vary with the size of the case of which he is a member. Workers from relief cases which had received large grants were employed at unskilled labor on the Program in substantially the same proportion as workers whose

---

[40] A case leaving relief and accepting Works Program employment was not designated as a Works Program closing until receipt of the first, full Works Program check. Inasmuch as payments were made twice a month in nearly all instances, Works Program closings for 1935 in the 13 cities do not include cases obtaining Works Program employment during the latter half of December 1935.

cases had received small relief grants, and the median wage rate
was about the same for each type of case (appendix table 70).

Occupational skills are classified on the Works Program as
unskilled, intermediate, skilled, and professional and technical.
Four-fifths of all jobs on the Program in December 1935 called
for unskilled workers.[41] Wages of the bulk of the workers were,
correspondingly, within narrow limits: the monthly wage rates[42]
of over three-fifths of the Program workers during the last
quarter of 1935 were within the interval $50—$59.[43] Relief
grants to these cases, though, during the last 30 days on relief,
were within broad limits; the greatest concentration, which
took in only a fourth of the cases, was of those receiving relief grants within the interval $20—$29 (appendix table 70).

The majority of the relief cases transferred to the Works
Program benefited considerably from the transfer. The average
relief grant to cases on relief throughout May 1935 ranged from
$10 for the one-person case to $61 for cases of eight persons
or more (appendix table 69). The Works Program wage rate exceeded the relief grant of the last 30 days on relief in 85 percent of the cases. In only 7 percent of the cases did the relief grant exceed the Works Program wage rate (appendix table
71). Works Program wage rates exceeded former relief grants
by at least $20 a month in about three-fourths of the cases
studied and by at least $40 a month in about one-third of the
cases. Two-thirds of the family cases and 98 percent of the
nonfamily cases had Works Program wage rates that exceeded their
relief grants by $20 a month or more.

There were, of course, cases in which relief grants exceeded
Works Program wage rates. In 4 percent of all cases the situation was reversed and the relief grants were the larger by $20
a month or more. Practically all of these were family cases

---

[41]Eighty percent of the workers employed on the Works Program in the
United States in December 1935 held unskilled jobs; corresponding proportions for June 1936 and May 1937 were 65 and 66 percent, respectively. See
reports on progress of the Works Program published by the Works Progress
Administration, Division of Statistics, Washington, D. C.

[42]Data on actual monthly income from Works Program employment are not
available from this study. Since the worker was paid for time lost because
of bad weather and other like conditions which were beyond his control, the
average monthly wage income was doubtless substantially the same as the average monthly wage rate.

[43]The present comparison of Works Program wage rates with former relief
grants includes data for all relief cases closed because of Works Program
employment in 13 cities during the last quarter of 1935 except those cases
which had both Works Program and private employment (6 percent of total
Works Program closings) and those in which the Works Program workers were
over 64 years of age (2 percent of total). Inasmuch as all kinds of employment financed under the Emergency Relief Appropriation Act of 1935
(including both CCC and NYA employment) came within the scope of the study,
a small number—approximately 1 percent—of the cases closed by Works Program employment had two members employed on the Program. In such cases,
the Works Program wage rate used in the analysis is the sum of the two rates.

(appendix table 72). The wage rates fell below the former relief grants in nearly a tenth of the family cases. In some cities this deficiency was offset in part by supplementing the Works Program wage with relief; in other cities wage rates were increased by as much as 10 percent.[44]

Private-Employment Income Compared With Former Relief Grants and With Works Program Wage Rates

The distribution of relief grants and wage rates about their respective averages differed sharply. Relief grants fell within comparatively broad limits because of varying needs according to size of case. Works Program wage rates, because of the predominance of unskilled jobs on the Program, fell within very narrow limits. Private-employment wage rates, without these controlling factors, fell within very broad limits.

Private-employment income, at time of closing, averaged nearly three times as much as the amount of relief granted during the last 30 days on relief.[45] The difference was a little smaller for family cases but much larger for nonfamily cases (appendix table 74). The average difference held for both white and Negro cases, but among Negro cases the average relief and the average private income was about a third less, in each instance, than that for whites.[46]

The average private-employment income was only a third greater than the average wage rate of cases transferred to the Works Program. There were wide differences, though, by race and size of case in variations from this average: the Works Program wage rate remained about the same for white, Negro, family, and nonfamily cases, but private-employment income was much higher for whites than for Negroes and for family cases than for nonfamily cases.

---

[44]Executive Order 7046 (May 20, 1935) authorized the Works Progress Administrator to adjust the "rate of earnings for any class of work in a locality by not more than 10 percent from the monthly earnings."

[45]Approximately 10 percent of the cases leaving the relief rolls with private employment had two or more members employed at the time of closing. The wage rate presented here for a given case is the sum of the wage rates of all its employed workers 16—64 years of age.

[46]Two facts may account for the difference between median relief grants to white and Negro cases. In the first place, Negro cases leaving the relief rolls were smaller than white cases. Negro cases leaving the relief rolls during 1935 averaged 2.2 persons a case as against 2.9 for whites. Negroes therefore required smaller relief grants. In the second place, average relief grants were smaller in the South than in the North. Inasmuch as Negroes constituted a larger proportion of total cases in the South than in the North, this lower relief grant in the South had greater effect upon the average for Negro cases than upon the average for white cases. Available evidence indicates that relief grants in the southern cities (Atlanta and Houston) included in this study were smaller for Negro cases of a given size than for white cases. In the remaining cities of the study there is no significant difference between relief grants to whites and Negroes by case size.

Half of the relief cases which had private employment at time of closing had wage rates of more than $80 a month; in contrast, only about a half of the relief cases with private employment had received more than $30 a month during the 30 days preceding the last relief grant. Nine-tenths of the relief cases had grants of less than $60 a month, while three-fourths of the cases on the Works Program had wage rates of less than this amount. But only a fifth of the private-employment wages were less than $60 (appendix tables 70 and 73).

Income from private employment was greater than the amount of relief formerly received in over 90 percent of all cases leaving the relief rolls with such employment. This condition prevailed for family and nonfamily cases and also for white cases. The corresponding proportion for Negro cases was about 85 percent.

Private-employment income exceeded former relief grants by $40 a month or more in nearly three-fourths of the cases, by $60 or more in almost one-half, and by at least $80 in nearly one-third of the cases. These differences were substantially the same for family, nonfamily, and white cases but were smaller for Negro cases (appendix table 75).

Relief grants exceeded private-employment income in a small proportion of the cases where such income was obviously insufficient to close the case; most of these were closed because of aid from relatives and friends and because of resources discovered by the agency.

Utilization of the Skills of Workers on the Works Program

Works Program jobs were concentrated largely in the unskilled category. This resulted from difficulties encountered in providing semiskilled, skilled, and white-collar work which would not compete with private industry and which would require only minimum outlays for equipment, materials, and nonrelief supervision. Unskilled jobs comprised more than four-fifths of all those on the Works Program held by experienced workers in relief cases in the 13 cities closed by December 31, 1935. In terms of their usual occupations, however, less than a half of these workers were in the unskilled group. This meant that white-collar, skilled, and semiskilled workers assigned to the Program had accepted jobs outside their usual occupations.

In view of occupational differences between whites and Negroes on relief, the proportion of employed Negroes on the Works Program holding unskilled jobs exceeded that of whites. Because of the placement of women in semiskilled work on Works Program sewing projects and because of the larger proportion of women among Negro workers than among white workers, the proportion of employed Negroes doing semiskilled work was greater than that of whites (appendix table 76).

Occupational Shifts

Comparatively few workers other than those in the unskilled group were assigned to Works Program jobs in their usual occupations. About nine-tenths of all unskilled workers assigned to the Program were given unskilled jobs; less than a third of all assigned white-collar workers were given white-collar work; and the proportions of all assigned skilled and semiskilled workers given jobs at their usual occupations were even smaller—a seventh and a tenth, respectively. Only a small percent of the experienced workers transferred from relief rolls in the 13 cities to the Works Program during 1935 held jobs in occupational levels higher than those in which they usually worked; the great bulk was rather evenly divided between those who held jobs in their usual occupational groups and those who had accepted jobs in an occupational level lower than that in which they usually worked. It should be noted, however, that white-collar workers, by definition, could not move upward in the occupational scale and that unskilled persons could not move downward. Of those who could move upward, only a small percent actually did so, but over three-fourths of those who could move downward accepted jobs in occupational levels lower than those of their usual employment. Nearly all of the downward movement was into unskilled work, since most of the Works Program jobs were in that category (appendix tables 76 and 77).

A somewhat greater proportion of Negroes than whites on the Works Program were assigned jobs at their usual occupations. This difference was due to two factors. First, more Negroes than whites on relief were unskilled workers, and transfers from relief to the Program approximated a cross section of the relief load. Second, most of the jobs on the Program, for either whites or Negroes, were unskilled. The transfer of the employable relief load to the Works Program, therefore, necessarily resulted in a greater occupational shift downward of white workers than of Negroes. Accordingly, about a half of all white workers transferred to the Program shifted downward, while slightly over a fourth of the Negro workers did so. Nearly all of this shift, for both racial groups, was into unskilled work.

Appendixes

Appendix A

SUPPLEMENTARY TABLES

Table 1.—Proportion of Persons in the General Population Receiving First Relief in 1935, by Age, Sex, and Race, 13 Cities

Age	Percent of general population				
	All persons[1]	Male	Female	White	Negro
All ages	2.0	2.2	1.9	[2]1.9	[3]3.8
Under 16 years	2.2	2.2	2.1	2.0	3.6
16—24 years	2.1	2.1	2.2	2.0	4.1
25—44 years	1.9	2.0	1.8	1.7	3.5
45—64 years	2.1	2.4	1.7	1.9	4.1
65 years and over	2.2	2.6	1.9	2.0	6.6

[1]Includes "other" races.
[2]White male, 2.0 percent; white female, 1.7 percent.
[3]Negro male and female, each 3.8 percent.

Table 2.—Proportion of White and Negro Persons Receiving Relief or Wage Assistance, by Age and Sex, 13 Cities, December 1934 and December 1935

Age and sex	Percent of general population					
	All races[1]		White		Negro	
	December 1934	December 1935	December 1934	December 1935	December 1934	December 1935
AGE						
All ages	14.0	12.5	11.6	10.3	35.4	32.5
Under 16 years	21.1	18.5	17.4	15.1	55.0	49.6
16—24 years	11.9	10.4	10.2	8.8	28.1	25.9
25—44 years	10.8	9.4	8.8	7.5	26.0	23.8
45—64 years	13.3	12.6	11.3	10.6	37.5	36.1
65 years and over	10.7	10.7	9.0	9.1	48.2	45.1
SEX						
Both sexes	14.0	12.5	11.6	10.3	35.4	32.5
Male	13.9	12.5	11.9	10.5	33.2	31.0
Female	14.1	12.5	11.4	10.0	37.6	34.0

[1]Includes "other" races.

43

Table 3.—Proportion of Families Receiving Relief or Wage Assistance in December 1934 and in December 1935, by Size of Case, 13 Cities

Size of case	Percent of general population	
	December 1934	December 1935
2 persons	12.7	12.9
3 persons	13.0	11.5
4 persons	13.5	11.3
5 persons	15.5	13.1
6 persons	15.2	13.2
7 persons	17.1	14.3
8 persons	18.5	15.7
9 persons	20.9	18.1
10 persons or more	22.9	20.9

Table 4.—Proportion of Experienced Workers Receiving Relief or Wage Assistance, by Usual Occupational Group, 13 Cities, December 1934 and December 1935

Usual occupational group	Percent of general population	
	December 1934	December 1935
Total	10.5	9.6
White-collar	4.4	4.4
Professional and technical	3.0	2.9
Managerial	3.8	4.1
Clerical	4.9	4.8
Skilled	9.1	7.7
Semiskilled	15.6	14.0
Unskilled	17.8	16.5
Manual	14.9	13.8
Domestic and personal service	22.0	20.4

Table 5.—Proportion of Experienced Workers Receiving Relief or Wage Assistance, by Usual Industrial Group, 13 Cities, December 1934 and December 1935

Usual industrial group	Percent of general population	
	December 1934	December 1935
Total	10.5	9.6
Building and construction	17.5	15.9
Iron and steel	10.4	8.5
Automobile	12.4	6.3
Transportation and communication	10.4	9.8
Food	13.5	15.6
Trade	6.6	6.4
Domestic and personal service	16.6	15.4
Miscellaneous	8.4	8.2

Table 6.—Trend of the Relief and Wage Assistance Load, by Cases, Persons, and Workers, 13 Cities, 1935

Month and year	Cases		Persons		Workers	
	Number	Percent	Number	Percent	Number	Percent
1934						
December	378,600	100.0	1,276,600	100.0	498,500	100.0
1935						
January	383,700	101.3	1,278,900	100.2	504,900	101.3
February	376,300	99.4	1,241,100	97.2	492,500	98.8
March	375,100	99.1	1,227,700	96.2	488,200	97.9
April	365,600	96.6	1,199,400	94.0	475,100	95.3
May	356,300	94.1	1,171,600	91.8	463,200	92.9
June	349,700	92.4	1,154,000	90.4	454,300	91.1
July	345,500	91.3	1,140,700	89.4	447,300	89.7
August	348,200	92.0	1,149,400	90.0	449,700	90.2
September	351,100	92.7	1,159,600	90.8	452,200	90.7
October	358,000	94.6	1,171,900	91.8	459,500	92.2
November	353,200	93.3	1,139,400	89.3	452,700	90.8
December	355,200	93.8	1,137,300	89.1	456,300	91.5

Table 7.—Persons Receiving Relief or Wage Assistance, by Age and Sex, 13 Cities, December 1934 and December 1935

Age	Male			Female		
	December 1934	December 1935	Percent change	December 1934	December 1935	Percent change
Total	641,400	573,100	−10.6	635,200	564,200	−11.2
Under 16 years	248,700	218,400	−12.2	242,500	213,100	−12.1
16—24 years	87,000	75,800	−12.9	92,400	81,600	−11.7
25—44 years	165,000	142,900	−13.4	187,600	163,500	−12.8
45—64 years	119,700	114,600	−4.3	91,900	85,700	−6.7
65 years and over	21,000	21,400	+1.9	20,800	20,300	−2.4

Table 8.—Trend in Age Distribution of Persons Receiving Relief or Wage Assistance, 13 Cities, December 1934—December 1935

Month and year	Age in years					
	Total	Under 16	16—24	25—44	45—64	65 and over
1934						
December	100.0	38.5	14.0	27.6	16.6	3.3
1935						
January	100.0	38.2	14.1	27.6	16.8	3.3
February	100.0	37.9	14.0	27.6	17.1	3.4
March	100.0	37.8	14.0	27.4	17.3	3.5
April	100.0	37.9	14.0	27.3	17.3	3.5
May	100.0	38.0	14.0	27.2	17.3	3.5
June	100.0	38.1	14.0	27.0	17.3	3.6
July	100.0	38.2	14.0	27.0	17.2	3.6
August	100.0	38.3	14.0	27.0	17.1	3.6
September	100.0	38.4	13.9	27.0	17.1	3.6
October	100.0	38.2	13.9	27.1	17.2	3.6
November	100.0	37.8	13.9	27.0	17.6	3.7
December	100.0	38.0	13.8	26.9	17.6	3.7
Average[1] 13 months	100.0	38.1	14.0	27.2	17.2	3.5
Average monthly change[2]	—	0.00	−0.02	−0.06	+0.05	+0.03

[1] Arithmetic mean.
[2] Representing the slope of the straight line trend fitted by least squares to the percents for each age group (see fig. 2).

Table 9.—Persons Receiving Relief or Wage Assistance, by Age and Race, and Sex and Race, 13 Cities, December 1934 and December 1935

Age and sex	White			Negro		
	December 1934	December 1935	Percent change	December 1934	December 1935	Percent change
Total _____	947,900	835,000	-11.9	303,800	278,900	-8.2
AGE						
Under 16 years _____	362,100	314,600	-13.1	116,000	104,700	-9.7
16—24 years _____	136,500	118,000	-13.6	40,400	37,300	-7.7
25—44 years _____	251,200	213,500	-15.0	94,500	86,200	-8.8
45—64 years _____	164,900	155,300	-5.8	44,700	43,000	-3.8
65 years and over _____	33,200	33,600	+1.2	8,200	7,700	-6.1
SEX						
Male _____	489,100	430,900	-11.9	139,100	129,800	-6.7
Female _____	458,800	404,100	-11.9	164,700	149,100	-9.5

Table 10.—Cases Receiving Relief or Wage Assistance, by Size of Case, 13 Cities, December 1934 and December 1935

Size of case	December 1934	December 1935
Total: Number_____	378,600	355,200
Percent_____	100.0	100.0
1 person_____	21.6	24.9
2 persons or more_____	78.4	75.1
2 persons_____	20.0	21.7
3 persons_____	17.6	16.5
4 persons_____	15.0	13.4
5 persons_____	10.8	9.8
6 persons_____	6.2	5.7
7 persons_____	3.8	3.4
8 persons or more_____	5.0	4.6
Average[1] number of persons a case_____	3.4	3.2

[1] Arithmetic mean.

Table 11.—Trend of the Relief and Wage Assistance Load, by Size of Case, 13 Cities, December 1934—December 1935

Month and year	Number of persons in case						
	Total cases	1 person	2 persons or more	2 persons	3 or 4 persons	5, 6, or 7 persons	8 persons or more
1934							
December: Number_____	378,600	81,700	296,900	75,800	123,600	78,600	18,900
Percent_____	100.0	100.0	100.0	100.0	100.0	100.0	100.0
1935							
January_____	101.3	104.6	101.7	103.2	99.8	99.0	99.6
February_____	99.4	104.8	100.2	103.2	97.1	94.5	96.4
March_____	99.1	106.4	100.1	104.4	95.8	92.4	95.3
April_____	96.6	103.0	97.4	102.3	93.0	90.5	93.9
May_____	94.1	98.8	94.9	100.8	91.0	88.4	91.8
June_____	92.4	96.1	93.0	98.9	89.4	87.5	90.6
July_____	91.3	94.7	91.9	97.5	88.3	86.9	88.7
August_____	92.0	95.2	92.6	98.7	88.9	87.6	89.2
September_____	92.7	96.0	93.3	99.3	89.5	88.9	89.5
October_____	94.6	100.6	95.4	101.8	90.4	89.2	89.6
November_____	93.3	103.9	94.6	101.5	87.2	85.6	86.5
December_____	93.8	108.1	95.2	101.9	86.0	85.1	87.1

Table 12.—Trend of Relief or Wage Assistance to Cases With Workers and Cases Without Workers, 13 Cities, December 1934—December 1935

Month and year	All cases	Type of case	
		Without worker	With worker
1934			
December: Number	378,600	38,900	339,700
Percent	100.0	100.0	100.0
1935			
January	101.3	101.3	101.3
February	99.4	100.9	99.2
March	99.1	102.8	98.6
April	96.6	100.8	96.1
May	94.1	98.9	93.6
June	92.4	98.3	91.7
July	91.3	97.1	90.6
August	92.0	97.6	91.3
September	92.7	98.2	92.1
October	94.6	99.9	94.0
November	93.3	100.1	92.5
December	93.8	99.4	93.2

Table 13.—Workers Receiving Relief or Wage Assistance, by Race, Sex, and Experience Status, 13 Cities, December 1934 and December 1935

Race, sex, and experience status	Number of workers		Percent change during year	Percent distribution	
	December 1934	December 1935		December 1934	December 1935
Total	498,500	456,300	-8.5	100.0	100.0
Male	347,000	315,300	-9.1	69.6	69.1
Female	151,500	141,000	-6.9	30.4	30.9
White	366,900	334,000	-9.0	73.6	73.2
Male	270,800	242,200	-10.6	54.3	53.1
Female	96,100	91,800	-4.5	19.3	20.1
Negro	124,400	115,300	-7.3	25.0	25.3
Male	70,500	67,500	-4.3	14.2	14.8
Female	53,900	47,800	-11.3	10.8	10.5
Other races	7,200	7,000	-2.8	1.4	1.5
Male	5,700	5,600	-1.8	1.1	1.2
Female	1,500	1,400	-6.7	0.3	0.3
Experienced	423,500	387,500	-8.5	85.0	84.9
Inexperienced	75,000	68,800	-8.3	15.0	15.1

Table 14.—Experienced Workers Receiving Relief or Wage Assistance, by Usual Occupational Group, 13 Cities, December 1934 and December 1935

Usual occupational group	Number of workers		Percent change during year	Percent distribution	
	December 1934	December 1935		December 1934	December 1935
Total	423,500	387,500	-8.5	100.0	100.0
White-collar	72,000	70,900	-1.5	17.0	18.3
Professional and technical	7,600	7,200	-5.3	1.8	1.9
Managerial	12,700	13,600	+7.1	3.0	3.5
Clerical	51,700	50,100	-3.1	12.2	12.9
Skilled	63,500	53,500	-15.7	15.0	13.8
Semiskilled	136,400	122,400	-10.3	32.2	31.6
Unskilled	151,600	140,700	-7.2	35.8	36.3
Manual	74,100	68,700	-7.3	17.5	17.7
Domestic and personal service	77,500	72,000	-7.1	18.3	18.6

Table 15.—Trend in Occupational Distribution of Experienced Workers Receiving Relief or Wage Assistance, 13 Cities, December 1934—December 1935

Month and year	Usual occupational group				
	Total	White-collar	Skilled	Semi-skilled	Unskilled
1934					
December	100.0	17.0	15.0	32.2	35.8
1935					
January	100.0	17.3	15.2	31.3	36.2
February	100.0	17.6	15.3	30.4	36.7
March	100.0	17.8	15.1	30.0	37.1
April	100.0	17.8	14.7	30.0	37.5
May	100.0	18.0	14.4	30.4	37.2
June	100.0	18.2	14.2	31.0	36.6
July	100.0	18.2	14.1	31.6	36.1
August	100.0	18.2	14.0	32.0	35.8
September	100.0	18.1	13.9	32.1	35.9
October	100.0	18.1	13.8	32.1	36.0
November	100.0	18.4	13.9	31.7	36.0
December	100.0	18.3	13.8	31.6	36.3
Average[1] 13 months	100.0	17.9	14.4	31.3	36.4
Average monthly change[2]	—	+0.10	−0.14	+0.09	−0.05

[1] Arithmetic mean.

[2] Representing the slope of the straight line trend fitted by least squares to the percents for each occupational group (see fig. 4).

Table 16.—Experienced Workers Receiving Relief or Wage Assistance, by Usual Industrial Group, 13 Cities, December 1934 and December 1935

Usual industrial group	Number of workers		Percent change during year	Percent distribution	
	December 1934	December 1935		December 1934	December 1935
Total	423,500	387,500	−8.5	100.0	100.0
Building and construction	48,400	44,100	−8.9	11.4	11.4
Iron and steel	27,900	22,800	−18.3	6.6	5.9
Automobile	33,200	16,900	−49.1	7.8	4.4
Transportation and communication	47,500	44,700	−5.9	11.2	11.5
Food	18,300	21,000	+14.8	4.3	5.4
Trade	59,100	57,600	−2.5	14.0	14.9
Domestic and personal service	87,400	81,300	−7.0	20.6	21.0
Miscellaneous	101,700	99,100	−2.6	24.1	25.5

Table 17.—Trend of Employment in the United States and of Experienced Workers Receiving Relief or Wage Assistance, by Usual Industrial Group, 13 Cities, December 1934—December 1935

Month and year	Usual industrial group								
	Total	Building and construction	Iron and steel	Automobile	Transportation and communication	Food	Trade	Domestic and personal service	Miscellaneous
Relief and wage assistance									
1934									
December	100.0	100.0	100.0	100.0	100.0	100.0	100.0	100.0	100.0
1935									
January	101.2	103.9	101.3	81.7	103.3	106.8	103.3	102.8	101.6
February	98.7	104.4	94.0	62.0	102.1	111.8	103.3	102.6	99.2
March	97.8	104.1	91.2	50.7	101.9	116.7	104.2	102.8	98.9
April	95.1	99.1	85.9	48.8	98.7	113.9	101.5	100.5	97.4
May	92.5	94.7	82.8	47.8	95.1	110.1	99.0	98.3	95.8
June	90.6	90.6	81.5	51.1	92.8	108.1	97.5	94.0	94.8
July	89.2	86.8	80.3	60.7	90.3	105.3	94.9	91.5	93.6
August	89.8	86.8	81.1	67.4	90.1	105.9	95.2	91.4	93.5
September	90.4	86.5	80.4	71.9	90.1	106.8	95.2	91.8	94.2
October	92.1	87.8	81.2	74.1	92.0	111.0	97.0	94.2	94.9
November	90.7	88.8	80.4	59.6	92.4	112.2	97.0	92.1	95.0
December	91.5	91.1	81.7	50.9	94.1	114.8	97.5	93.0	97.4
Employment[1]									
1934									
December	100.0	100.0	100.0	100.0	100.0	100.0	100.0	100.0	100.0
1935									
January	100.7	88.1	100.6	112.4	93.7	95.2	103.6	101.2	100.9
February	99.1	77.6	102.5	122.9	89.5	87.1	98.3	102.3	100.8
March	100.1	74.6	106.8	128.9	88.7	86.6	98.5	103.8	102.2
April	100.6	76.9	108.5	131.6	88.8	85.5	99.0	104.7	102.3
May	101.4	85.3	109.8	133.1	92.1	87.5	100.4	104.6	101.6
June	101.5	94.9	109.4	132.0	95.5	87.9	99.6	104.4	101.0
July	101.5	99.3	108.5	127.4	97.8	90.8	99.4	104.1	100.6
August	101.6	100.7	107.7	124.8	98.6	97.0	98.1	104.3	101.2
September	102.4	104.3	110.6	121.5	98.8	102.6	97.7	104.5	102.7
October	103.4	107.1	112.9	113.5	96.4	108.5	99.6	104.5	104.6
November	104.4	107.1	115.5	125.1	95.8	99.5	100.9	105.0	105.7
December	104.3	99.3	116.0	130.6	93.3	92.2	101.6	106.1	105.8

[1] All employment figures shown are actually those for the preceding month.

Table 18.—Cases Admitted to the Relief Rolls, by Type of Accession, 13 Cities, 1935

Type of accession	Percent distribution				
	Year	1st quarter	2d quarter	3d quarter	4th quarter
Total accessions	100	100	100	100	100
Reopened cases	56	49	57	61	58
New cases	44	51	43	39	42
With prior relief in other cities	7	7	8	6	6
Without prior relief anywhere	37	44	35	33	36

Table 19.—Monthly Accession and Separation Rates of Cases, Persons, and Workers Receiving Relief or Wage Assistance, 13 Cities, 1935

Month	Accession rate (percent)			Separation rate (percent)		
	Cases	Persons	Workers	Cases	Persons	Workers
Average for year	5.0	4.3	4.9	5.6	5.3	5.6
January	6.3	5.2	6.4	4.9	5.1	5.2
February	5.2	4.3	5.2	7.2	7.3	7.7
March	5.2	4.4	5.0	5.5	5.5	5.9
April	2.9	2.7	2.9	5.5	5.0	5.6
May	2.8	2.5	2.8	5.3	4.8	5.3
June	4.4	3.9	4.2	6.3	5.4	6.1
July	5.8	5.1	5.5	7.0	6.3	7.0
August	6.2	5.6	5.8	5.4	4.8	5.3
September	5.6	5.1	5.2	4.8	4.2	4.7
October	5.9	4.9	5.5	4.0	3.8	3.9
November	5.0	3.9	4.6	6.4	6.8	6.1
December	5.3	4.5	5.2	4.7	4.7	4.4

Table 20.—Average Monthly Accession and Separation Rates of Relief Persons, by Age and Sex, Age and Race, and Sex and Race, 13 Cities, January—December 1935

Description	Accession rate (percent)			Separation rate (percent)		
Age by sex						
	Total	Male	Female	Total	Male	Female
All ages	4.3	4.6	4.1	5.3	5.5	5.1
Under 16 years	3.9	3.9	3.9	5.0	5.0	5.0
16—24 years	4.8	4.8	4.7	5.9	6.0	5.8
25—44 years	4.9	5.6	4.3	6.1	6.9	5.5
45—64 years	4.1	4.4	3.6	4.5	4.8	4.2
65 years and over	3.8	4.0	3.5	3.8	3.8	3.7
Age by race						
	Total[1]	White	Negro	Total	White	Negro
All ages	4.3	4.9	2.7	5.3	6.0	3.4
Under 16 years	3.9	4.6	2.2	5.0	5.8	3.0
16—24 years	4.8	5.4	2.9	5.9	6.6	3.6
25—44 years	4.9	5.6	3.2	6.1	7.0	4.0
45—64 years	4.1	4.5	2.6	4.5	5.0	2.9
65 years and over	3.8	4.1	2.5	3.8	4.0	3.1
Sex by race						
	Total[1]	White	Negro	Total	White	Negro
Both sexes	4.3	4.9	2.7	5.3	6.0	3.4
Male	4.6	5.1	2.9	5.5	6.2	3.5
Female	4.1	4.7	2.5	5.1	5.8	3.3

[1] Includes "other" races amounting to about 2 percent of the total number of persons on relief.

Table 21.—Average Monthly Accession and Separation Rates of Relief Cases, by Size of Case, 13 Cities, January—December 1935

Size of case	Accession rate (percent)	Separation rate (percent)
All sizes	5.0	5.6
1 person	7.5	6.8
2 persons	4.7	4.6
3 persons	4.6	5.7
4 persons	4.3	5.8
5 persons	3.9	5.3
6 persons	4.1	5.3
7 persons	3.7	5.2
8 persons or more	3.5	4.9

Table 22.—Average Monthly Accession and Separation Rates of All Workers on Relief, by Sex and Race, 13 Cities, 1935

Sex	Accession rate (percent)			Separation rate (percent)		
	Total[1]	White	Negro	Total[1]	White	Negro
Both sexes	4.9	5.4	3.3	5.6	6.2	3.9
Male	5.1	5.6	3.5	6.0	6.6	3.9
Female	4.2	5.0	2.9	4.8	5.3	3.9

[1]Includes "other" races amounting to less than 2 percent of all workers on relief.

Table 23.—Average Monthly Accession and Separation Rates of Experienced Workers on Relief, by Usual Occupational Group, 13 Cities, 1935

Usual occupational group	Accession rate (percent)	Separation rate (percent)
Total	5.1	5.9
White-collar	4.9	5.0
Professional and technical	5.1	5.6
Managerial	5.7	5.1
Clerical	4.6	4.9
Skilled	5.1	6.6
Semiskilled	5.5	6.5
Unskilled	4.8	5.5
Manual	5.6	6.3
Domestic and personal service	4.1	4.7

Table 24.—Monthly Accession Rates of Experienced Workers on Relief, by Usual Industrial Group, 13 Cities, 1935

Month	Total	Building and construction	Iron and steel	Automobile	Transportation and communication	Food	Trade	Domestic and personal service	All others
					Percent				
Average for year	5.1	4.4	4.5	7.6	4.8	6.4	5.0	4.3	5.7
January	6.6	6.9	5.8	3.5	7.0	10.1	7.3	6.0	7.0
February	5.4	5.8	4.3	3.0	5.4	9.9	6.1	5.2	5.1
March	5.2	4.5	3.7	5.2	5.0	8.7	6.0	4.6	5.4
April	3.0	1.7	1.9	3.6	2.6	3.4	2.8	2.5	4.5
May	2.9	1.7	2.3	4.4	2.5	2.6	2.7	2.3	4.2
June	4.4	2.8	4.1	11.3	4.2	4.9	4.4	3.2	5.4
July	5.8	4.0	5.5	23.3	4.9	5.5	4.8	4.4	5.9
August	6.2	5.2	6.2	15.5	5.3	6.4	5.4	4.9	6.4
September	5.6	4.3	4.9	11.3	4.6	6.1	4.9	4.6	6.4
October	5.9	5.0	5.2	8.4	5.5	7.7	5.5	5.8	5.9
November	4.9	4.7	4.7	3.4	5.2	5.9	4.8	4.2	5.7
December	5.4	6.3	5.8	4.4	6.1	6.1	5.1	4.1	6.1

Table 25.—Monthly Separation Rates of Experienced Workers on Relief, by Usual Industrial Group, 13 Cities, 1935

Month	Total	Building and construction	Iron and steel	Automobile	Transportation and communication	Food	Trade	Domestic and personal service	All others
					Percent				
Average for year	5.9	5.2	6.3	14.1	5.4	5.2	5.2	4.9	5.9
January	5.4	3.0	4.5	21.8	3.8	3.3	3.9	3.2	5.4
February	7.9	5.3	11.5	27.1	6.6	5.1	6.1	5.5	7.5
March	6.0	4.8	6.6	23.5	5.2	4.3	5.2	4.4	5.6
April	5.8	6.5	7.7	7.2	5.7	5.8	5.4	4.7	6.0
May	5.6	6.2	6.0	6.6	6.2	5.9	5.1	4.5	5.8
June	6.6	7.1	5.6	4.4	6.6	6.7	5.8	7.6	6.4
July	7.3	8.2	7.1	4.5	7.7	8.1	7.5	7.1	7.2
August	5.5	5.5	5.3	4.3	5.5	5.8	5.1	5.0	6.6
September	4.9	4.3	5.7	4.7	4.6	5.2	4.9	4.2	5.7
October	4.0	3.6	4.2	5.4	3.4	3.7	3.6	3.2	5.1
November	6.5	3.6	5.7	23.9	4.7	4.8	4.9	6.4	5.7
December	4.5	3.5	4.0	23.4	4.0	3.5	4.5	3.0	3.6

Table 26.—Reason for Opening Relief Cases, 13 Cities, 1935

Reason	All cases			Family cases			Nonfamily cases		
	Total[1]	White	Negro	Total[1]	White	Negro	Total[1]	White	Negro
10 months: March—December									
All reasons	177,287	143,078	31,889	117,768	97,432	19,132	59,519	45,646	12,757
Works Program openings	4,340	3,644	588	4,134	3,445	582	206	199	6
Loss of job	983	844	133	788	127		195	189	6
Insufficient earnings	3,357	2,800	455	3,346	2,790	455	11	10	—
Regular openings: Number	172,947	139,434	31,301	113,634	93,987	18,550	59,313	45,447	12,751
Percent	100.0	100.0	100.0	100.0	100.0	100.0	100.0	100.0	100.0
Loss of private employment	55.2	57.3	46.1	61.0	62.8	51.6	44.2	45.8	38.1
Within 30 days	24.9	26.1	19.6	27.2	28.2	21.9	20.5	21.8	16.2
More than 1 but less than 4 months	30.3	31.2	26.5	33.8	34.6	29.7	23.7	24.0	21.9
Decreased hours or pay	6.5	6.1	8.0	7.9	7.6	9.7	3.7	3.2	5.6
Depletion of resources	14.1	14.8	10.8	13.4	13.9	10.8	15.4	16.6	10.7
Strike	0.7	0.8	0.1	0.9	1.1	0.1	0.3	0.3	*
Increased needs	0.9	0.8	1.2	0.9	0.8	1.5	0.8	0.8	0.9
Other reasons	22.6	20.2	33.8	15.9	13.8	26.3	35.6	33.3	44.7
5 months: August—December									
All reasons	100,579	80,371	18,857	65,776	53,973	11,121	34,803	26,398	7,736
Works Program openings	4,340	3,644	588	4,134	3,445	582	206	199	6
Loss of job	983	844	133	788	655	127	195	189	6
Insufficient earnings	3,357	2,800	455	3,346	2,790	455	11	10	—
Regular openings: Number	96,239	76,727	18,269	61,642	50,528	10,539	34,597	26,199	7,730
Percent	100.0	100.0	100.0	100.0	100.0	100.0	100.0	100.0	100.0
Loss of private employment	56.2	58.7	45.0	62.1	64.4	50.6	45.8	47.8	37.5
Within 30 days	24.1	25.6	17.6	26.6	27.8	20.6	19.6	21.5	13.5
More than 1 but less than 4 months	32.1	33.1	27.4	35.5	36.6	30.0	26.2	26.3	24.0
Decreased hours or pay	6.5	6.0	8.5	7.9	7.3	10.5	4.0	3.6	5.6
Depletion of resources	11.3	12.1	8.2	11.1	11.7	8.5	11.6	12.7	7.9
Strike	0.6	0.7	*	0.8	0.9	0.1	0.2	0.2	—
Increased needs	0.8	0.8	1.1	0.9	0.8	1.5	0.6	0.7	0.5
Other reasons	24.6	21.7	37.2	17.2	14.9	28.8	37.8	35.0	48.5
Aid from friends, relatives, etc	16.8	14.5	26.7	11.3	9.8	18.8	26.6	23.5	37.6
Loss of financial aid	0.1	0.1	0.1	0.1	0.1	*	0.1	0.1	0.1
Loss of regular Government employment	0.5	0.6	0.4	0.4	0.5	0.5	0.6	0.7	0.2
Emergency needs	0.4	0.4	0.4	0.5	0.5	0.5	0.2	0.2	0.2
Discharged from institution	1.2	1.1	1.4	0.1	0.1	0.1	3.2	3.3	3.1
Administrative policy	2.1	1.6	4.3	2.1	1.5	4.8	2.1	1.7	3.7
Investigation completed	1.6	1.4	2.5	1.5	1.2	3.1	1.8	1.9	1.7
Transferred from other agency	1.1	1.2	0.8	1.0	1.0	0.8	1.4	1.6	0.7
Miscellaneous	0.8	0.8	0.6	0.2	0.2	0.2	1.8	2.0	1.2

*Less than 0.05 percent.

[1]Includes "other" races.

141777 O—39——5

Table 27.—Reason For Opening New Relief Cases, 13 Cities, 1935

Reason	All cases			Family cases			Nonfamily cases		
	Total[1]	White	Negro	Total[1]	White	Negro	Total[1]	White	Negro
10 months: March—December									
All reasons	72,609	56,188	15,375	41,090	32,883	7,784	31,519	23,305	7,591
Works Program openings	53	48	5	21	17	4	32	31	1
Loss of job	48	44	4	16	13	3	32	31	1
Insufficient earnings	5	4	1	5	4	1	—	—	—
Regular openings: Number	72,556	56,140	15,370	41,069	32,866	7,780	31,487	23,274	7,590
Percent	100.0	100.0	100.0	100.0	100.0	100.0	100.0	100.0	100.0
Loss of private employment	46.6	48.1	41.6	52.3	53.5	47.1	39.2	40.3	35.9
Within 30 days	17.4	18.3	14.1	19.2	19.8	16.5	15.0	16.2	11.7
More than 1 but less than 4 months	29.2	29.8	27.5	33.1	33.7	30.6	24.2	24.1	24.2
Decreased hours or pay	5.6	5.3	6.8	7.2	6.9	8.8	3.6	3.2	4.9
Depletion of resources	18.8	20.6	12.0	18.0	19.5	11.7	19.9	22.1	12.2
Strike	1.0	1.2	0.1	1.5	1.8	0.2	0.2	0.3	*
Increased needs	0.7	0.6	1.0	0.8	0.6	1.3	0.5	0.5	0.7
Other reasons	27.3	24.2	38.5	20.2	17.7	30.9	36.6	33.6	46.3
5 months: August—December									
All reasons	38,691	29,394	8,780	20,860	16,563	4,095	17,831	12,831	4,685
Works Program openings	53	48	5	21	17	4	32	31	1
Loss of job	48	44	4	16	13	3	32	31	1
Insufficient earnings	5	4	1	5	4	1	—	—	—
Regular openings: Number	38,638	29,346	8,775	20,839	16,546	4,091	17,799	12,800	4,684
Percent	100.0	100.0	100.0	100.0	100.0	100.0	100.0	100.0	100.0
Loss of private employment	47.2	48.9	41.1	53.6	55.0	48.0	39.6	41.1	35.1
Within 30 days	16.3	17.6	12.1	18.5	19.3	15.6	13.7	15.4	9.1
More than 1 but less than 4 months	30.9	31.3	29.0	35.1	35.7	32.4	25.9	25.7	26.0
Decreased hours or pay	5.7	5.3	7.0	7.2	6.6	9.4	3.3	3.6	4.8
Depletion of resources	16.1	18.1	9.4	16.2	17.9	9.5	16.0	18.4	9.3
Strike	0.6	0.7	*	0.8	1.1	*	0.2	0.2	—
Increased needs	0.6	0.6	0.9	0.9	0.6	1.2	0.5	0.4	0.6
Other reasons	29.8	26.4	41.6	21.3	18.8	31.9	39.8	36.3	50.2
Aid from friends, relatives, etc	23.5	20.6	33.9	16.2	14.5	23.6	32.1	28.4	43.0
Loss of financial aid	0.1	0.1	0.1	*	0.1	*	0.1	0.1	0.1
Loss of regular Government employment	0.2	0.2	0.1	0.1	0.1	0.1	0.3	0.4	*
Discharged from institution	1.1	1.0	1.2	0.1	0.1	0.1	2.3	2.3	2.3
Administrative policy	2.6	2.0	4.6	2.8	1.8	6.5	2.4	2.3	3.0
Transferred from other agency	1.7	1.9	0.9	1.8	2.0	1.2	1.5	1.8	0.6
Miscellaneous	0.6	0.6	0.8	0.3	0.2	0.4	1.1	1.0	1.2

*Less than 0.05 percent.

[1] Includes "other" races.

Table 28.—Reason for Reopening Relief Cases, 13 Cities, 1935

Reason	All cases			Family cases			Nonfamily cases		
	Total[1]	White	Negro	Total[1]	White	Negro	Total[1]	White	Negro
10 months: March—December									
All reasons _____	104,678	86,890	16,514	76,678	64,549	11,348	28,000	22,341	5,166
Works Program reopenings _____	4,287	3,596	583	4,113	3,428	578	174	168	5
Loss of job _____	935	800	129	772	642	124	163	158	5
Insufficient earnings _____	3,352	2,796	454	3,341	2,786	454	11	10	—
Regular reopenings: Number _____	100,391	83,294	15,931	72,565	61,121	10,770	27,826	22,173	5,161
Percent _____	100.0	100.0	100.0	100.0	100.0	100.0	100.0	100.0	100.0
Loss of private employment _____	61.5	63.5	50.6	65.9	67.8	54.9	50.0	51.6	41.5
Within 30 days _____	30.3	31.4	24.9	31.7	32.7	25.8	26.7	27.7	22.9
More than 1 but less than 4 months _____	31.2	32.1	25.7	34.2	35.1	29.1	23.3	23.9	18.6
Decreased hours or pay _____	7.1	6.7	9.1	8.3	7.9	10.3	3.9	3.2	6.7
Depletion of resources _____	10.6	10.9	9.6	10.8	11.0	10.2	10.2	10.8	8.5
Strike _____	0.5	0.5	*	0.5	0.6	0.1	0.3	0.3	*
Increased needs _____	1.1	1.0	1.5	1.1	0.9	1.6	1.1	1.2	1.1
Other reasons _____	19.2	17.4	29.2	13.4	11.8	22.9	34.5	32.9	42.2
5 months: August—December									
All reasons _____	61,888	50,977	10,077	44,916	37,410	7,026	16,972	13,567	3,051
Works Program reopenings _____	4,287	3,596	583	4,113	3,428	578	174	168	5
Loss of job _____	935	800	129	772	642	124	163	158	5
Insufficient earnings _____	3,352	2,796	454	3,341	2,786	454	11	10	—
Regular reopenings: Number _____	57,601	47,381	9,494	40,803	33,982	6,448	16,798	13,399	3,046
Percent _____	100.0	100.0	100.0	100.0	100.0	100.0	100.0	100.0	100.0
Loss of private employment _____	62.3	64.8	48.6	66.4	69.0	52.2	52.3	54.1	41.1
Within 30 days _____	29.3	30.6	22.7	30.7	31.9	23.8	25.9	27.3	20.3
More than 1 but less than 4 months _____	33.0	34.2	25.9	35.7	37.1	28.4	26.4	26.8	20.8
Decreased hours or pay _____	7.0	6.5	9.8	8.2	7.7	11.2	4.1	3.6	6.8
Depletion of resources _____	8.1	8.4	7.2	8.5	8.7	7.9	6.9	7.4	5.7
Strike _____	0.5	0.6	0.1	0.7	0.8	0.1	0.2	0.2	—
Increased needs _____	1.0	0.9	1.3	1.1	0.9	1.7	0.8	0.9	0.5
Other reasons _____	21.1	18.8	33.0	15.1	12.9	26.9	35.7	33.8	45.9
Loss of aid from friends, relatives, etc _____	12.3	10.7	20.1	8.8	7.4	15.8	20.7	19.0	29.4
Loss of financial aid _____	0.1	0.1	0.1	0.1	0.1	0.1	*	*	*
Loss of regular Government employment _____	0.7	0.8	0.6	0.6	0.7	0.7	0.9	1.1	0.5
Emergency needs _____	0.6	0.6	0.7	0.8	0.7	0.9	0.4	0.4	0.4
Discharged from institution __	1.3	1.2	1.5	0.1	0.1	0.1	4.3	4.2	4.5
Administrative policy _____	1.8	1.3	4.1	1.7	1.4	3.7	1.8	1.1	4.9
Investigation completed _____	2.6	2.3	1.8	2.2	1.7	5.0	3.7	3.6	4.3
Transferred from other agency _	0.8	0.8	0.6	0.6	0.6	0.5	1.3	1.4	0.8
Miscellaneous _____	0.9	1.0	0.5	0.2	0.2	0.1	2.6	3.0	1.1

*Less than 0.05 percent.

[1] Includes "other" races.

Table 29.—Reason for Closing Relief Cases, 13 Cities, 1935

Reason	All cases			Family cases			Nonfamily cases		
	Total[1]	White	Negro	Total[1]	White	Negro	Total[1]	White	Negro
10 months: March—December									
All reasons	345,886	266,051	75,105	257,869	197,754	56,915	88,017	68,297	18,190
Works Program closings	151,821	110,173	39,313	120,449	86,485	32,224	31,372	23,688	7,089
Regular closings: Number	194,065	155,878	35,792	137,420	111,269	24,691	56,645	44,609	11,101
Percent	100.0	100.0	100.0	100.0	100.0	100.0	100.0	100.0	100.0
Private employment	50.8	54.1	36.8	62.3	66.1	45.3	23.1	24.2	17.8
Increased hours or pay	7.0	7.1	6.6	9.1	9.3	8.5	1.9	1.8	2.6
Client failed to report	13.3	13.4	12.5	4.6	4.2	6.5	34.3	36.3	25.6
Resources discovered	4.4	4.1	5.8	5.0	4.6	6.5	3.1	2.8	4.4
Strike or lockout ended	0.2	0.2	0.1	0.3	0.3	0.1	0.1	*	0.2
Decreased needs	0.5	0.5	0.5	0.4	0.4	0.4	0.6	0.6	0.8
Other reasons	23.8	20.6	37.7	18.3	15.1	32.7	36.9	34.3	48.6
5 months: August—December									
All reasons	238,395	180,347	54,770	183,327	137,640	43,335	55,068	42,707	11,435
Works Program closings	151,811	110,164	39,312	120,439	86,476	32,223	31,372	23,688	7,089
Regular closings: Number	86,584	70,183	15,458	62,888	51,164	11,112	23,696	19,019	4,346
Percent	100.0	100.0	100.0	100.0	100.0	100.0	100.0	100.0	100.0
Private employment	53.8	57.5	36.9	64.3	68.6	44.4	25.9	27.4	17.5
Increased hours or pay	6.2	6.4	5.5	7.9	8.2	7.0	1.7	1.7	1.7
Client failed to report	9.0	8.9	9.2	3.8	3.3	5.8	22.7	23.9	17.9
Resources discovered	1.9	2.0	1.7	2.1	2.1	1.9	1.6	1.7	1.3
Strike or lockout ended	0.4	0.4	0.1	0.5	0.6	0.1	*	*	0.1
Decreased needs	0.4	0.4	0.3	0.3	0.3	0.2	0.6	0.6	0.8
Other reasons	28.3	24.4	46.3	21.1	16.9	40.6	47.5	44.7	60.7
Aid from friends, relatives, etc	6.2	4.9	12.3	4.7	3.4	11.1	10.3	9.1	15.3
Financial aid	3.6	3.7	3.3	3.6	3.7	3.2	3.7	3.8	3.5
Change of residence	4.3	4.4	3.5	2.9	3.2	1.9	7.8	7.8	7.7
Death	1.1	1.0	1.5	*	*	*	4.0	3.8	5.2
Marriage	0.3	0.3	0.2	0.3	0.3	0.3	0.3	0.4	0.2
Institutionalization	1.9	1.9	1.8	0.1	0.1	0.2	6.5	6.7	6.0
Administrative policy	3.8	3.4	5.7	2.7	2.4	4.2	6.8	6.2	9.3
Refusal of employment	0.5	0.5	0.6	0.5	0.4	0.8	0.5	0.6	0.2
Expectancy of Works Program employment	2.5	0.4	12.3	2.9	0.4	14.2	1.5	0.2	7.3
Transferred to other agency	2.3	2.2	2.9	1.9	1.7	2.7	3.6	3.7	3.3
Pensions	0.5	0.5	0.3	0.4	0.3	0.4	0.8	0.9	0.1
Miscellaneous	1.3	1.2	1.9	1.1	1.0	1.6	1.7	1.5	2.6

*Less than 0.05 percent.

[1]Includes "other" races.

Table 30.—Reason for Opening Family and Nonfamily Relief Cases,[1] 13 Cities,
March—December 1935

Reason	March	April	May	June	July	August	September	October	November	December
Family cases	100.0	100.0	100.0	100.0	100.0	100.0	100.0	100.0	100.0	100.0
Loss of private employment	49.1	58.0	55.2	62.9	70.6	65.0	66.7	58.0	58.1	60.8
Within 30 days	21.0	29.3	30.2	32.3	29.3	29.6	26.5	24.4	27.0	24.7
More than 1 but less than 4 months	28.1	28.7	25.0	30.6	41.3	35.4	40.2	33.6	31.1	36.1
Decreased hours or pay	8.0	8.7	8.7	7.5	7.4	6.7	7.1	8.3	8.9	9.0
Loss or depletion of resources	23.5	19.1	18.5	12.1	9.4	9.3	9.6	12.6	13.2	12.0
Other reasons	19.4	14.2	17.6	17.5	12.6	19.0	16.6	21.1	19.8	18.2
Loss of aid from friends, relatives, etc							11.1	9.7	13.2	12.1	10.4
Administrative policy and transfers							3.5	5.3	2.3	2.1	2.2
Miscellaneous							4.4	1.6	5.6	5.6	5.6
Nonfamily cases	100.0	100.0	100.0	100.0	100.0	100.0	100.0	100.0	100.0	100.0
Loss of private employment	38.7	37.8	39.8	43.9	47.9	39.8	38.1	44.7	51.1	53.4
Within 30 days	23.6	18.7	21.5	22.0	21.3	17.7	16.7	20.1	22.7	20.2
More than 1 but less than 4 months	15.1	19.1	18.3	21.9	26.6	22.1	21.4	24.6	28.4	33.2
Decreased hours or pay	3.2	2.9	2.9	2.7	4.4	4.4	4.5	3.5	3.9	4.0
Loss or depletion of resources	25.1	28.9	30.4	14.4	11.7	12.9	12.1	10.6	11.5	11.2
Other reasons	33.0	30.4	26.9	39.0	36.0	42.9	45.3	41.2	33.5	31.4
Loss of aid from friends, relatives, etc							29.3	29.0	27.6	24.7	23.0
Administrative policy and transfers							8.0	9.2	6.5	5.2	5.3
Miscellaneous							5.6	7.1	7.1	3.6	3.1

[1]Excludes relief cases opened because of insufficient Works Program income or loss of Works Program job.

Table 31.—Reason for Closing Family and Nonfamily Relief Cases, Works Program Closings
Excluded, 13 Cities, March—December 1935

Reason	March	April	May	June	July	August	September	October	November	December
Family cases	100.0	100.0	100.0	100.0	100.0	100.0	100.0	100.0	100.0	100.0
Private employment	70.3	62.4	58.0	55.0	56.6	56.3	55.9	62.7	69.3	75.0
Increased hours or pay	8.4	10.2	12.3	11.3	9.3	9.1	9.3	8.7	6.4	7.0
Client failed to report	4.4	5.9	4.9	5.3	6.1	4.6	5.5	4.7	2.3	2.9
Outside sources of income	8.5	11.1	11.4	10.1	8.8	7.6	9.0	7.1	2.8	3.6
Resources discovered						2.8	3.3	2.7	1.1	1.1
Financial aid						4.8	5.7	4.4	1.7	2.5
Other reasons	8.4	10.4	13.4	18.3	19.2	22.4	20.3	16.8	19.2	11.5
Aid from friends, relatives, etc						6.1	5.1	5.4	4.0	3.5
Expectancy of Works Program employment						—	—	0.4	9.6	0.5
Change of residence						4.0	3.9	2.6	1.9	2.7
Administrative policy						4.6	3.9	2.4	1.2	1.8
Transfers						2.9	3.8	4.0	1.0	1.0
Miscellaneous						4.8	3.6	2.0	1.5	2.0
Nonfamily cases	100.0	100.0	100.0	100.0	100.0	100.0	100.0	100.0	100.0	100.0
Private employment	22.0	22.9	16.4	21.6	23.1	23.7	22.3	29.5	28.1	28.2
Increased hours or pay	2.1	1.8	1.7	2.3	2.4	1.6	1.7	1.7	1.8	1.5
Client failed to report	46.7	45.4	52.1	40.8	30.7	28.1	26.0	19.9	16.8	19.2
Outside sources of income	5.5	6.2	5.4	5.6	5.8	6.0	5.7	4.8	5.4	4.0
Resources discovered						1.0	1.8	1.6	1.6	2.2
Financial aid						5.0	3.9	3.2	3.8	1.8
Other reasons	23.7	23.7	24.4	29.7	38.0	40.6	44.3	44.1	47.9	47.1
Aid from friends, relatives, etc						9.0	9.6	11.4	11.7	10.2
Expectancy of Works Program employment						—	—	0.3	7.7	0.2
Change of residence						6.3	7.8	10.2	7.1	8.4
Administrative policy						9.2	8.4	5.2	4.0	5.4
Transfers						10.2	11.7	10.3	11.6	10.5
Miscellaneous						5.9	6.8	6.6	5.8	12.4

Table 32.—Reason for Closing Relief Cases Without Workers 16 Through 64 Years of Age, by Race, 13 Cities, May and October 1935

Reason	Total[1]		White		Negro	
	May	October	May	October	May	October
Total: Number	1,510	1,403	1,221	1,091	286	296
Percent	100.0	100.0	100.0	100.0	100.0	100.0
Aid from friends, relatives, etc	20.1	20.6	18.0	19.1	29.6	26.8
Outside sources of income	24.1	12.8	27.2	14.0	10.9	9.2
Transfers to agencies or institutions	9.8	16.0	8.6	15.9	14.4	16.6
Deceased	11.5	10.9	8.8	9.1	23.2	17.6
Change of address	6.1	8.1	6.9	8.9	2.5	5.1
Administrative policy and ruling	7.2	4.1	7.0	4.1	8.5	4.4
Private employment	6.8	7.1	7.9	8.6	2.1	2.0
Works Program employment	—	6.9	—	7.0	—	6.4
All other specified reasons	2.8	6.1	3.3	6.5	0.7	3.4
Unknown	11.6	7.4	12.3	6.8	8.1	8.5

[1]Total includes a few cases of "other" races.

Table 33.—Experienced and Inexperienced Workers in Regular Closings, by Race and Employment Status, 13 Cities, July—December 1935

Type	Number of workers in regular closings		Percent distribution		Employed workers for every 1,000 workers
	Total workers	Employed workers	Total workers	Employed workers	
ALL RACES[1]					
Total	139,678	74,356	100.0	100.0	532
Experienced	123,231	72,226	88.2	97.1	586
Inexperienced	16,447	2,130	11.8	2.9	130
WHITE					
Total	112,928	62,475	100.0	100.0	553
Experienced	98,628	60,508	87.3	96.9	613
Inexperienced	14,300	1,967	12.7	3.1	138
NEGRO					
Total	25,260	10,908	100.0	100.0	432
Experienced	23,315	10,881	92.3	99.8	467
Inexperienced	1,945	27	7.7	0.2	14

[1]Includes "other" races.

Table 34.—Usual Occupational Group of Workers on Relief and Usual and Current Occupational Group of Workers Having Private Employment at Closing, by Race, 13 Cities, July—December 1935

Usual occupational group	Average monthly worker load	Workers having private employment at closing					
		All races[1]		White		Negro	
		Usual employment	Current employment	Usual employment	Current employment	Usual employment	Current employment
Total: Number	383,800	72,226	72,226	60,508	60,508	10,881	10,881
Percent	100.0	100.0	100.0	100.0	100.0	100.0	100.0
White-collar	18.2	14.5	13.7	16.5	15.4	4.3	4.8
Skilled	13.9	17.5	14.8	19.6	16.6	6.7	5.2
Semiskilled	31.9	36.8	36.0	39.5	38.4	23.0	24.1
Unskilled	36.0	31.2	35.5	24.4	29.6	66.0	65.9

[1]Includes "other" races.

Table 35.—Usual Occupational Group of Employed Workers, by Occupational Group of Private Employment at Time of Regular Closing and by Race, 13 Cities, July—December 1935

Usual occupational group	Employed workers		Occupational group of current employment					
	Number	Percent	White-collar	Skilled	Semi-skilled	Unskilled		
						Total	Manual	Domestic and personal service
ALL RACES[1]								
Experienced	72,226	100.0	13.7	14.8	36.0	35.5	22.7	12.8
White-collar	10,489	100.0	71.0	4.1	13.1	11.8	6.7	5.1
Skilled	12,656	100.0	5.1	70.1	13.3	11.5	9.0	2.5
Semiskilled	26,586	100.0	4.0	3.5	80.1	12.4	8.4	4.0
Unskilled	22,495	100.0	3.4	1.9	7.4	87.3	54.7	32.6
Manual	14,195	100.0	3.3	2.1	7.5	87.1	84.2	2.9
Domestic and personal service	8,300	100.0	3.7	1.4	7.2	87.7	4.4	83.3
Inexperienced	2,130	100.0	29.8	1.0	34.8	34.4	15.4	19.0
Unknown	74	100.0	31.1	—	31.1	37.8	14.8	23.0
WHITE								
Experienced	60,508	100.0	15.4	16.6	38.4	29.6	21.1	8.5
White-collar	9,957	100.0	71.6	4.1	12.9	11.4	6.6	4.8
Skilled	11,876	100.0	5.2	70.6	13.1	11.1	8.7	2.4
Semiskilled	23,893	100.0	4.2	3.8	80.6	11.4	7.9	3.5
Unskilled	14,782	100.0	4.0	2.4	7.5	86.1	62.2	23.9
Manual	10,652	100.0	3.4	2.4	7.0	87.2	84.8	2.4
Domestic and personal service	4,130	100.0	5.6	2.2	8.9	83.3	4.0	79.3
Inexperienced	1,967	100.0	31.2	1.0	36.1	31.7	14.5	17.2
Unknown	59	100.0	35.6	—	32.2	32.2	18.6	13.6
NEGRO								
Experienced	10,881	100.0	4.8	5.2	24.1	65.9	29.4	36.5
White-collar	468	100.0	59.4	3.4	18.0	19.2	10.3	8.9
Skilled	730	100.0	4.0	62.3	16.4	17.3	13.4	3.9
Semiskilled	2,505	100.0	2.0	1.0	75.3	21.7	12.5	9.2
Unskilled	7,178	100.0	2.4	0.9	7.3	89.4	38.2	51.2
Manual	3,140	100.0	3.2	1.3	9.6	85.9	81.3	4.6
Domestic and personal service	4,038	100.0	1.7	0.6	5.5	92.2	4.7	87.5
Inexperienced	27	100.0	15.7	0.8	20.5	63.0	17.3	45.7
Unknown	15	100.0	13.3	—	26.7	60.0	—	60.0

[1]Includes "other" races.

Table 36.—Usual Industrial Group of Workers on Relief and Usual and Current Industrial Group of Workers Having Private Employment at Time of Regular Closing, by Race, 13 Cities, June—September 1935

Usual industrial group	Average monthly relief load	Workers having private employment at closing					
		All races[1]		White		Negro	
		Usual employment	Current employment	Usual employment	Current employment	Usual employment	Current employment
Total: Number	450,900	49,395	49,395	40,204	40,204	8,485	8,485
Percent	100.0	100.0	100.0	100.0	100.0	100.0	100.0
Building and construction	11.3	13.1	12.4	14.3	13.6	7.8	6.9
Iron and steel	5.9	5.9	6.0	6.0	6.2	5.3	5.1
Automobile	4.9	3.7	3.3	4.2	3.7	1.4	1.4
Transportation and communication	11.4	10.1	9.6	10.3	9.8	9.1	8.4
Food	5.1	5.7	5.3	5.9	5.5	4.5	4.4
Trade	14.9	14.1	14.1	15.1	15.2	10.0	9.9
Domestic and personal service	21.4	17.7	19.5	11.1	12.9	48.7	50.5
Miscellaneous	25.1	29.7	29.8	33.1	33.1	13.2	13.4

[1]Includes "other" races.

Table 37.—Shift From Usual Industrial Group by Workers Having Private Employment at Time of Regular Closing, 13 Cities, June—September 1935

Usual industrial group	Percent employed outside usual industry		
	All races[1]	White	Negro
All industries	26.4	27.6	20.3
Building and construction	25.1	23.9	33.6
Iron and steel	35.7	36.9	27.4
Automobile	38.3	38.3	38.5
Transportation and communication	39.0	39.0	36.5
Food	34.9	36.5	25.4
Trade	34.0	33.3	38.9
Domestic and personal service	14.1	20.0	7.3
Miscellaneous	21.4	20.9	28.7

[1]Includes "other" races amounting to less than 2 percent of the total employed workers in separations.

Table 38.—Usual Industrial Group of Employed Workers, by Industrial Group of Employment at Time of Regular Closing and by Race, 13 Cities, June—September 1935

Usual industrial group	Employed workers[1]		Industrial group of current employment							
	Number	Per-cent	Building and con-struction	Iron and steel	Auto-mobile	Transpor-tation and communi-cation	Food	Trade	Domestic and personal service	Miscel-laneous
ALL RACES[2]										
Total	49,395	100.0	12.4	6.0	3.3	9.6	5.3	14.1	19.5	29.8
Building and construction	6,454	100.0	74.9	2.2	1.2	4.8	1.8	5.0	2.7	7.4
Iron and steel	2,916	100.0	3.9	64.3	1.9	5.4	1.4	6.8	3.2	13.1
Automobile	1,832	100.0	5.7	6.5	61.7	5.5	2.1	5.7	4.4	8.4
Transportation and communica-tion	5,013	100.0	4.9	3.7	2.3	61.0	3.0	8.0	5.6	11.5
Food	2,812	100.0	3.0	2.5	0.6	4.1	65.1	7.1	7.1	11.1
Trade	6,909	100.0	3.2	2.5	1.3	5.0	2.4	66.0	7.3	12.3
Domestic and personal service	8,748	100.0	0.9	0.7	0.4	1.7	0.8	4.2	85.9	5.4
Miscellaneous	14,631	100.0	2.8	2.3	0.8	3.4	1.5	5.5	5.1	78.6
WHITE										
Total	40,204	100.0	13.6	6.2	3.7	9.8	5.5	15.2	12.9	33.1
Building and construction	5,750	100.0	76.1	2.2	1.3	4.3	1.8	4.9	2.1	7.3
Iron and steel	2,416	100.0	4.4	63.1	2.0	5.4	1.6	6.6	3.1	13.8
Automobile	1,706	100.0	5.6	6.7	61.7	5.7	2.1	5.4	4.0	8.8
Transportation and communica-tion	4,132	100.0	4.9	3.5	2.6	61.0	3.2	8.3	4.4	12.1
Food	2,368	100.0	3.2	2.8	0.7	4.4	63.5	6.6	7.1	11.7
Trade	6,087	100.0	3.2	2.6	1.2	4.7	2.6	66.7	6.1	12.9
Domestic and personal service	4,460	100.0	1.2	1.2	0.5	2.1	1.3	5.8	80.0	7.9
Miscellaneous	13,285	100.0	2.8	2.1	0.9	3.5	1.3	5.6	4.7	79.1
NEGRO										
Total	8,485	100.0	6.9	5.1	1.4	8.4	4.4	9.9	50.5	13.4
Building and construction	658	100.0	66.4	2.6	0.6	6.4	2.0	5.8	7.7	8.5
Iron and steel	453	100.0	1.8	72.6	0.9	3.7	0.7	8.2	3.5	8.6
Automobile	122	100.0	7.4	3.3	61.5	2.5	2.4	9.8	10.7	2.4
Transportation and communica-tion	772	100.0	5.0	3.8	0.9	63.5	1.7	7.0	11.9	6.2
Food	378	100.0	1.3	0.5	0.3	2.4	74.6	6.4	7.1	7.4
Trade	844	100.0	3.3	1.2	2.5	6.9	0.8	61.1	15.9	8.3
Domestic and personal service	4,135	100.0	0.6	0.1	0.1	1.4	0.3	2.5	92.7	2.3
Miscellaneous	1,123	100.0	3.3	3.4	0.2	2.9	3.5	4.8	10.6	71.3

[1]Excludes persons whose usual or current industry is unknown.
[2]Includes "other" races.

Table 39.—Proportion of Cases Admitted to the Relief Rolls Having I Person or More Employed at Time of Opening,[1] by Race, 13 Cities, 1935

Month	Total intake			New cases			Reopened cases		
	Total[2]	White	Negro	Total[2]	White	Negro	Total[2]	White	Negro
	Percent								
Average for year --	12.3	11.9	14.5	10.1	9.4	12.6	14.1	13.7	16.3
January	14.1	13.6	16.7	12.0	11.1	16.0	16.1	15.9	17.5
February	14.6	14.1	16.3	12.5	11.5	16.2	16.7	16.7	16.4
March	12.7	12.4	14.1	9.0	8.7	10.1	16.6	15.9	19.5
April	12.0	11.6	15.1	10.8	10.2	14.6	13.1	12.7	15.7
May	[3]13.2	12.9	14.7	10.0	9.6	12.6	15.7	15.4	16.6
June	12.5	12.5	12.7	9.9	9.4	12.2	14.2	14.5	13.1
July	11.3	11.4	11.2	9.2	8.9	10.7	12.7	12.9	11.6
August	11.6	11.0	14.4	9.4	8.9	11.1	13.0	12.2	17.0
September	11.8	10.9	15.3	9.8	9.0	11.9	13.0	11.9	18.1
October	12.8	12.2	15.4	9.4	8.6	12.0	15.1	14.4	18.4
November	11.7	10.7	15.4	9.3	8.0	13.6	13.3	12.3	17.5
December	10.0	9.9	10.8	7.9	7.5	9.3	11.0	11.1	12.0

[1]Excludes cases which, because of strike or temporary layoff, had no private employment income.

[2]All races are included in this total. Whites and Negroes constitute more than 98 percent of all cases admitted to relief in 13 cities during the year.

[3]The comparable proportion of supplemented cases in the total relief load for May 1935 in these cities was 13.4 percent, according to a sample survey taken.

Table 40.—Proportion of Cases on Relief Also Having Private Employment, by Size of Case, in 13 Cities, May 1935, and in 12 Cities and 79 Cities, May 1934

Size of case	May 1935, 13 cities[1]			Percent of cases with private employment, May 1934[2]	
	All cases	Cases with private employment		12 cities	79 cities
		Number	Percent		
All sizes	8,576	1,148	13.4	18.9	17.6
1 person	1,924	88	4.6	7.9	5.9
2 persons	1,841	226	12.3	15.4	13.2
3 persons	1,474	217	14.7	18.9	17.5
4 persons	1,232	199	16.2	20.7	19.8
5 persons	879	144	16.4	23.7	22.2
6 persons	500	96	19.2	26.8	24.0
7 persons	304	60	19.7	31.9	28.7
8 persons	183	44	24.0	32.6	29.8
9 persons	115	33	28.7	36.7	33.0
10 persons or more	124	41	33.1	39.1	39.5

[1]Carmichael, F. L. and Payne, Stanley L., *The 1935 Relief Population in 13 Cities: A Cross-Section*, Research Bulletin Series I, No. 23, Division of Social Research, Works Progress Administration, December 31, 1936, p. 14. This study of the May 1935 relief population was based upon a sample ranging from 1 percent of the total load in Chicago to approximately 10 percent in the smaller cities. The aggregate (14,174 cases) constituted 4 percent of the May 1935 relief load. Each city was assigned a weight based upon the relation of its relief load to the relief load of the 13 cities. The weights so determined for the 13 cities were then adjusted, by application of a constant factor, to yield a weighted aggregate of 10,000 cases. Of this number 1,066 cases were on relief only a part of May and 358 cases did not report supplementation status. The remainder (8,576 cases), on relief throughout May, were distributed by case size as shown here.

[2]Occupational Characteristics Survey conducted as of May 1934 by the Division of Social Research, Works Progress Administration. With 1 exception (Omaha) the 13 cities on which the present report is based were included in the 79 cities surveyed. Data for these 12 cities are shown in the 12-city column. Data on the 79 cities surveyed are published in the study by Palmer, Gladys L. and Wood, Katherine D., *Urban Workers on Relief*, Part I—The Occupational Characteristics of Workers on Relief in Urban Areas May 1934, Research Monograph IV, Division of Social Research, Works Progress Administration, Washington, D. C., 1936, p. 61.

Note: The May 1934 and the May 1935 tabulations differ in 2 important respects. First, the May 1934 tabulation includes all cases on the relief rolls at some time during the month, while the May 1935 tabulation is limited to cases which were on relief throughout the month. Second, in the May 1934 tabulation cases with members on strike were regarded as having private employment, whereas in the May 1935 tabulation such cases (without earnings from any source) were not regarded as having private employment.

Table 41.—Average[1] Monthly Relief Benefit to Supplemented and Nonsupplemented Cases on Relief Throughout May 1935, by Size of Case, 13 Cities

Size of case	Nonsupplemented cases	Supplemented cases	Ratio of supplemented case benefit to nonsupplemented case benefit (percent)
Total cases reporting	7,408	1,142	
All sizes	$28	[1]$22	79
1 person	13	10	77
2 persons	22	18	82
3 persons	29	22	76
4 persons	33	27	82
5 persons	40	30	75
6 persons	44	36	82
7 persons	51	41	80
8 persons	56	43	77
9 persons	60	44	73
10 persons or more	73	57	78

[1]This is a "standardized" average. It was derived by weighting the average relief grants of supplemented cases of a given size by the number of nonsupplemented cases of the same size. Such weighting, made necessary by the overrepresentation of large cases in the supplemented group, yields an average which is directly comparable with the average for the nonsupplemented group. The unweighted average of the supplemented cases is $27.

Table 42.—Average[1] Monthly Income of Supplemented and Nonsupplemented Cases on Relief Throughout May 1935, by Size of Case, 13 Cities

Size of case	Relief of nonsupplemented cases	Income of supplemented cases			Ratio of income of supplemented cases to relief of nonsupplemented cases (percent)		
		Total[2]	Relief grants	Nonrelief earnings	Total[2]	Relief grants	Nonrelief earnings
All sizes	$28	$42	$22	$20	150	79	71
1 person	13	20	10	10	154	77	77
2 persons	22	34	18	16	155	82	73
3 persons	29	42	22	20	145	76	69
4 persons	33	54	27	27	164	82	82
5 persons	40	59	30	29	147	75	72
6 persons	44	66	36	30	150	82	68
7 persons	51	70	41	29	137	80	57
8 persons	56	79	43	36	141	77	64
9 persons	60	84	44	40	140	73	67
10 persons or more	73	99	57	42	136	78	58

[1]Arithmetic mean.

[2]Relief grants and nonrelief earnings only; income from other sources is disregarded.

Note: Relief-grant and private-employment income averages for supplemented cases, presented in this table for all case sizes combined, are standardized averages. They were derived by weighting the average for a given case size by the number of nonsupplemented cases of the same size. The unweighted averages for supplemented cases are: relief grants, $27; private-employment income, $24; relief-grant and private-employment income, $51. The weighted averages—$22, $20, and $42, respectively—are directly comparable with the average relief grant of nonsupplemented cases ($28).

Table 43.—Portion of Nonrelief Earnings Accruing to Supplemented Cases as Income in Excess of the Relief Grant to Nonsupplemented Cases on Relief Throughout May 1935, 13 Cities[1]

Size of case	Average monthly income			Average monthly nonrelief earnings of supplemented cases		
	Supplemented cases	Nonsupple-mented cases	Difference[2]	Total	Portion accruing as additional income to case	
					Amount[2]	Percent
All cases _____	$42	$28	$14	$20	$14	70
1 person _____	20	13	7	10	7	70
2 persons _____	34	22	12	16	12	75
3 persons _____	42	29	13	20	13	65
4 persons _____	54	33	21	27	21	78
5 persons _____	59	40	19	29	19	66
6 persons _____	66	44	22	30	22	73
7 persons _____	70	51	19	29	19	66
8 persons _____	79	56	23	36	23	64
9 persons _____	84	60	24	40	24	60
10 persons or more _____	99	73	26	42	26	62

[1]See note to table 42.
[2]Amount by which total monthly income of supplemented case exceeds that of nonsupplemented case.

Table 44.—Proportion of Experienced Workers in Relief Accessions Who Were Employed at Time of Opening, by Race and Sex, 13 Cities, 1935

Race and sex	Experienced workers		
	Total	Employed	
		Number	Percent
ALL RACES[1]			
Total_____	245,990	31,968	13.0
Male_____	189,602	19,599	10.3
Female_____	56,388	12,369	21.9
WHITE			
Total_____	198,939	25,220	12.7
Male_____	158,786	16,179	10.2
Female_____	40,153	9,041	22.5
NEGRO			
Total_____	43,890	6,441	14.7
Male_____	27,990	3,178	11.4
Female_____	15,900	3,263	20.5

[1]Includes "other" races.

Table 45.—Occupational Group of Jobs Held by Workers Employed While on Relief, by Race, in 12 Cities and 79 Cities, May 1934, and Relief Accessions in 13 Cities, 1935

Occupational group	Jobs held by workers on relief, May 1934		Jobs held by workers admitted to relief, 13 cities, 1935		
	12 cities	79 cities	All races[1]	White	Negro
	Percent distribution				
Total	100.0	100.0	[2]100.0	100.0	100.0
White-collar	20.3	17.7	22.1	24.6	12.5
Professional and technical	2.3	1.5	1.8	1.9	1.7
Managerial	4.1	3.7	7.2	7.0	8.0
Clerical	13.9	12.5	13.1	15.7	2.8
Skilled	13.1	9.1	6.7	7.9	2.1
Semiskilled	30.1	28.9	36.3	41.0	18.9
Unskilled	36.5	44.3	34.9	26.5	66.5
Manual	12.3	17.9	13.7	12.7	16.7
Domestic and personal service	24.2	26.4	21.2	13.8	49.8

[1]Includes "other" races.
[2]Based upon 31,763 jobs.

Table 46.—Industrial Group of Jobs Held by Workers Employed While on Relief, by Race, in 12 Cities and 79 Cities, May 1934, and Relief Accessions in 13 Cities, 1935

Industrial group	Jobs held by workers on relief, May 1934		Jobs held by workers admitted to relief, 13 cities, 1935		
	12 cities	79 cities	All races[1]	White	Negro
	Percent distribution				
Total	100.0	100.0	[2]100.0	100.0	100.0
Building and construction	5.0	4.5	2.9	3.4	1.2
Iron and steel	4.3	4.0	3.9	4.1	2.9
Automobile	3.8	2.3	2.8	3.3	1.1
Transportation and communication	7.6	8.0	7.2	7.5	6.0
Food	3.8	3.4	5.2	5.7	3.0
Trade	18.5	15.2	20.5	21.5	16.8
Domestic and personal service	24.3	30.6	27.0	19.3	56.9
Miscellaneous	32.7	32.0	30.5	35.2	12.1

[1]Includes "other" races.
[2]Based on 31,036. Excludes workers who did not report current industry.

Table 47.—Duration of **Unemployment** of Experienced Workers in Relief Accessions and Separations, by Race, 13 Cities, 1935

| Duration of unemployment | Accessions[1] | | | Separations[2] | | | | | |
| | | | | Regular | | | Works Program | | |
	All races[3]	White	Negro	All races[3]	White	Negro	All races[3]	White	Negro
All experienced workers_	214,444	174,096	37,495	237,701	191,213	43,790	168,040	118,927	46,669
Duration unknown_____	737	629	102	15,730	13,686	1,749	770	605	156
Duration known: Number_____	213,707	173,467	37,393	221,971	177,527	42,041	167,270	118,322	46,513
Percent_____	100.0	100.0	100.0	100.0	100.0	100.0	100.0	100.0	100.0
Less than 4.6 weeks_____	24.1	24.9	20.4	2.0	2.2	1.3	1.0	1.1	1.0
4.6—9.5 weeks_____	21.2	21.5	19.7	6.9	7.4	5.0	1.6	1.8	1.1
9.6—17.5 weeks_____	15.1	14.7	16.7	14.2	15.2	9.9	3.5	3.7	3.0
17.6—26.5 weeks_____	7.3	6.9	9.1	13.4	13.8	11.6	5.5	5.8	4.8
26.6—52.5 weeks_____	9.8	9.6	11.0	22.7	22.8	21.6	13.3	13.7	12.5
52.6—104.5 weeks_____	7.5	7.3	8.6	17.2	15.5	24.0	24.2	22.6	28.1
104.6—156.5 weeks_____	4.5	4.4	4.9	9.0	8.3	12.3	15.6	14.7	17.7
156.6—208.5 weeks_____	3.7	3.7	3.7	6.5	6.4	7.1	12.1	12.3	11.5
208.6—520 weeks_____	6.8	7.0	5.9	8.1	8.4	7.2	23.2	24.3	20.3

[1]Excludes those employed at opening.
[2]Excludes those continuously employed for at least 4 weeks prior to closing.
[3]All races includes a relatively small number of "other" races.

Table 48.—Average[1] Duration of Unemployment of Workers Admitted to Relief, by Race, Age, and Sex, 13 Cities, February—May 1935

| Race and age | Workers[2] in all cases | | | Workers[2] in new cases | | | Workers[2] in reopened cases | | |
	Total	Male	Female	Total	Male	Female	Total	Male	Female
	Average[1] unemployment duration in months								
ALL RACES[3]									
Total _____	3.3	3.0	5.5	3.8	3.5	5.3	2.9	2.4	5.7
16—24 years _____	3.9	3.4	5.7	3.9	3.5	5.5	3.9	3.3	5.9
25—34 years _____	2.8	2.3	5.9	3.4	2.9	5.8	2.2	2.0	6.0
35—44 years _____	3.0	2.6	5.1	3.6	3.3	5.0	2.3	2.1	5.2
45—54 years _____	3.6	3.4	5.2	3.9	3.8	4.7	3.3	3.1	6.2
55—64 years _____	5.0	5.1	4.4	5.8	6.1	4.2	4.1	4.1	4.6
WHITE									
Total _____	3.3	3.0	5.7	3.8	3.6	5.6	2.8	2.3	5.7
16—24 years _____	3.9	3.4	5.7	3.9	3.5	5.5	3.8	3.2	5.8
25—34 years _____	2.7	2.2	6.4	3.3	2.9	6.0	2.1	2.0	7.3
35—44 years _____	2.8	2.4	5.1	3.5	3.3	5.0	2.2	2.1	5.2
45—54 years _____	3.6	3.4	5.7	4.1	3.9	5.9	3.2	3.0	5.3
55—64 years _____	5.3	5.4	5.1	6.4	6.6	5.7	4.1	4.1	4.1
NEGRO									
Total _____	3.5	3.0	5.1	3.5	3.1	4.8	3.5	2.9	5.6
16—24 years _____	4.2	3.5	6.0	3.9	3.3	5.6	5.3	4.4	7.2
25—34 years _____	3.3	2.5	5.2	3.6	2.8	5.5	2.8	2.1	4.6
35—44 years _____	3.5	2.9	5.2	3.5	3.1	5.0	3.5	2.7	5.4
45—54 years _____	3.4	3.3	3.9	3.2	3.2	3.1	3.8	3.4	7.7
55—64 years _____	3.5	3.6	3.2	3.2	3.5	2.2	3.9	3.6	5.6

[1]Median.
[2]Unemployed experienced persons 16—64 years of age who were seeking work at time of relief opening.
[3]Includes "other" races amounting to less than 2 percent of total admissions to relief.

Table 49.—Average[1] Duration of Unemployment of Workers Admitted to Relief, by Race and Usual Occupational Group, 13 Cities, January—December 1935

Race	Usual occupational group[2]				
	Total	White-collar	Skilled	Semiskilled	Unskilled
Average[1] unemployment duration in months					
All races[3] ------------------------------	2.8	3.7	2.4	2.4	2.9
White -----------------------------------	2.6	3.7	2.4	2.3	2.6
Negro -----------------------------------	3.3	3.7	2.5	3.2	3.4

[1]Median.
[2]Unemployed experienced persons 16—64 years of age who were seeking work at time of relief opening.
[3]Includes "other" races amounting to less than 2 percent of total admissions to relief.

Table 50.—Duration of Unemployment of Workers Securing Jobs at Closing, Regular and Works Program Closings, 13 Cities, October—December 1935

Duration of unemployment	Percent distribution	
	Employed on Works Program	Employed in private industry
Total _____	100.0	100.0
Less than 1 month_____	0.7	1.9
1—1.9 months_____	1.1	8.2
2—2.9 months_____	1.8	14.7
3—3.9 months_____	1.9	10.4
4—4.9 months_____	2.8	11.5
5—5.9 months_____	2.6	7.9
6—8.9 months_____	5.9	9.9
9—11.9 months_____	6.5	5.8
12—14.9 months_____	7.4	4.9
15—17.9 months_____	6.3	4.0
18—20.9 months_____	5.3	2.5
21—23.9 months_____	5.4	2.8
24—29.9 months_____	9.3	3.5
30—35.9 months_____	5.8	1.9
36—41.9 months_____	6.9	2.7
42—47.9 months_____	5.9	2.1
48—59.9 months_____	11.9	2.6
60—71.9 months_____	8.2	1.7
72—95.9 months_____	3.9	0.8
96—119.9 months_____	0.4	0.2

Table 51.—Average[1] Duration of Unemployment of Experienced Workers in Regular and Works Program Closings, by Race, Sex, and Age, 13 Cities, October—December 1935

Race and sex	Age in years						
	Total	16—19	20—24	25—34	35—44	45—54	55—64
REGULAR CLOSINGS Average[1] duration of unemployment (in months) of all experienced workers							
ALL RACES							
Total ----------	8.1	9.0	8.4	6.8	7.0	10.3	14.5
Male ----------------	6.5	9.3	6.1	5.5	5.8	9.2	13.6
Female --------------	15.8	8.7	16.1	18.4	15.3	16.7	20.2
WHITE							
Total ----------	6.9	7.6	7.0	5.9	5.8	9.2	14.1
Male ----------------	6.1	8.7	5.8	5.3	5.5	8.7	14.1
Female --------------	12.0	6.9	12.1	15.6	11.6	13.0	14.3
NEGRO							
Total ----------	14.8	14.7	15.8	13.1	14.8	16.6	18.4
Male ----------------	8.7	10.8	8.4	5.9	9.7	11.9	10.5
Female --------------	20.6	17.8	22.0	19.8	19.8	22.7	23.9
OTHER							
Total ----------	12.2	13.5	8.3	14.1	12.9	12.6	11.0
Male ----------------	12.4	†	8.1	14.1	13.3	13.0	10.9
Female --------------	10.5	†	†	†	†	†	†
WORKS PROGRAM CLOSINGS Average[1] duration of unemployment (in months) of all experienced workers							
ALL RACES							
Total ----------	25.1	12.1	19.5	22.9	25.0	28.4	33.9
Male ----------------	25.7	11.1	19.2	22.4	25.3	28.9	35.8
Female --------------	23.0	12.9	20.1	24.7	23.8	25.9	23.0
WHITE							
Total ----------	25.5	11.5	18.4	22.5	25.5	29.3	36.5
Male ----------------	26.3	10.5	18.0	22.3	25.8	29.8	37.9
Female --------------	22.1	12.1	19.7	23.5	23.8	24.5	23.3
NEGRO							
Total ----------	24.2	16.3	21.8	23.4	24.1	26.5	28.3
Male ----------------	24.3	13.6	22.4	22.5	24.2	26.2	29.4
Female --------------	24.2	19.8	20.9	25.5	23.9	27.0	22.3
OTHER							
Total ----------	23.6	8.5	16.8	22.3	22.4	29.5	32.5
Male ----------------	24.1	8.0	17.3	20.6	23.8	29.3	32.5
Female --------------	17.2	9.0	16.5	54.0	4.8	36.6	—

† Median not computed because of small number of workers involved.

[1] Median.

[2] Excludes those continuously employed for at least 4 weeks prior to closing.

Table 52.—Average[1] Duration of Unemployment of All Workers and for Workers Securing Jobs, Regular and Works Program Closings, by Age, Race, and Sex, 13 Cities, October—December 1935

Age, race, and sex	Type of closing			
	Works Program closing		Regular closing	
	All workers	Workers securing jobs	All workers	Workers securing jobs
Number of workers	164,646	138,320	[2]48,699	[2]30,388
Average[1] unemployment duration in months				
AGE				
All ages				
Total	25.1	25.5	8.1	5.4
16—19 years	12.1	12.0	9.0	6.6
20—24 years	19.5	19.4	8.4	5.4
25—34 years	22.9	22.2	6.8	5.1
35—44 years	25.0	24.9	7.0	5.2
45—54 years	28.4	28.5	10.3	6.3
55—64 years	33.9	33.6	14.5	8.6
RACE AND SEX				
All races[3]				
Total	25.1	25.5	8.1	5.4
Male	25.7	25.9	6.5	5.2
Female	23.0	22.3	15.8	9.9
White				
Total	25.5	26.3	6.9	5.3
Male	26.3	26.6	6.1	5.1
Female	22.1	23.1	12.0	8.9
Negro				
Total	24.2	23.8	14.8	5.8
Male	24.3	24.2	8.7	5.5
Female	24.2	20.7	20.6	13.9

[1]Median.

[2]Excludes 6,913 workers continuously employed for at least 4 weeks prior to closing.

[3]Includes "other" races amounting to less than 2 percent of the total.

Table 53.—Average[1] Duration of Unemployment of Employed Workers in Regular and Works Program Closings, by Race, Sex, and Age, 13 Cities, October—December 1935

Race and sex	Age in years						
	Total	16—19	20—24	25—34	35—44	45—54	55—64

REGULAR CLOSINGS
Average[1] duration of unemployment (in months) of experienced workers who secured private employment at closing

Race and sex	Total	16—19	20—24	25—34	35—44	45—54	55—64
ALL RACES							
Total _____	·5.4	6.6	5.4	5.1	5.2	6.3	8.6
Male _____	5.2	6.3	5.1	4.9	5.0	6.1	8.6
Female _____	9.9	6.7	11.0	10.8	10.6	9.8	7.7
WHITE							
Total _____	5.3	5.9	5.1	5.0	5.0	5.9	8.8
Male _____	5.1	5.8	4.9	4.9	4.9	5.9	9.1
Female _____	8.9	6.0	9.7	11.3	9.0	9.1	5.0
NEGRO							
Total _____	5.8	12.5	7.0	5.2	5.7	10.8	4.8
Male _____	5.5	7.5	5.8	4.9	5.4	10.6	4.7
Female _____	13.9	22.5	26.3	9.7	14.0	18.0	23.3
OTHER							
Total _____	11.9	†	7.9	13.7	13.9	9.4	10.7
Male _____	11.9	†	7.9	13.9	14.1	9.8	10.6
Female _____	12.0	†	†	†	†	†	†

WORKS PROGRAM CLOSINGS
Average[1] duration of unemployment (in months) of experienced workers who secured Works Program employment at closing

Race and sex	Total	16—19	20—24	25—34	35—44	45—54	55—64
ALL RACES							
Total _____	25.5	12.0	19.4	22.2	24.9	28.5	33.6
Male _____	25.9	11.7	19.6	22.2	25.2	28.9	34.8
Female _____	22.3	12.6	18.1	22.0	22.9	24.0	23.2
WHITE							
Total _____	26.3	11.3	18.2	22.2	25.5	29.5	36.1
Male _____	26.6	10.8	18.1	22.3	25.7	29.8	37.1
Female _____	23.1	12.2	18.5	21.8	24.0	25.5	23.9
NEGRO							
Total _____	23.8	14.7	21.7	22.1	23.7	25.6	26.2
Male _____	24.2	13.9	22.2	22.2	24.2	26.1	29.1
Female _____	20.7	30.0	15.0	21.4	21.0	19.4	21.2
OTHER							
Total _____	24.5	†	18.7	20.6	23.3	31.1	31.7
Male _____	23.8	†	18.3	19.6	23.7	30.0	31.7
Female _____	37.9	†	†	99.2	†	†	—

†Median not computed on a base of fewer than 25 cases.

[1]Median.

141777 O—39——6

Table 54.—Duration of Unemployment for Experienced Workers Securing Employment at Closing, Regular and Works Program Closings, by Sex and Race, 13 Cities, October—December 1935

Duration of unemployment	Total	Sex		Race		
		Male	Female	White	Negro	Other
Regular closings						
All experienced persons with an unemployment period---	30,388	27,622	2,766	26,177	3,889	322
Duration not reported[1]_____	242	202	40	231	11	—
Duration reported: Number_____	30,146	27,420	2,726	25,946	3,878	322
Percent_____	100.0	100.0	100.0	100.0	100.0	100.0
Less than 6 months_____	54.6	56.3	36.4	55.3	51.7	24.8
6—11.9 months_____	15.7	15.4	19.8	15.9	14.2	25.5
12—23.9 months_____	14.2	13.7	20.9	13.6	17.7	31.7
24—35.9 months_____	5.4	5.0	9.1	5.0	7.6	6.8
36—47.9 months_____	4.8	4.6	5.9	4.9	3.5	8.4
48—59.9 months_____	2.6	2.6	2.4	2.6	3.0	0.3
60—119.9 months_____	2.7	2.4	5.5	2.7	2.3	2.5
Works Program closings						
All experienced persons with an unemployment period___	138,320	127,499	10,821	99,553	36,599	2,168
Duration not reported[1]_____	688	547	141	546	133	9
Duration reported: Number_____	137,632	126,952	10,680	99,007	36,466	2,159
Percent_____	100.0	100.0	100.0	100.0	100.0	100.0
Less than 6 months_____	10.9	10.8	11.0	11.2	10.0	7.3
6—11.9 months_____	12.4	12.5	12.2	12.7	11.8	11.7
12—23.9 months_____	24.4	23.9	31.1	22.7	28.9	30.3
24—35.9 months_____	15.1	14.7	19.3	14.6	16.6	12.4
36—47.9 months_____	12.8	13.0	10.9	13.0	12.2	14.4
48—59.9 months_____	11.9	12.3	6.6	12.4	10.5	12.2
60—119.9 months_____	12.5	12.8	8.9	13.4	10.0	11.7

[1]Includes experienced persons with employment status unknown as well as experienced employed persons with unemployment duration unknown.

Table 55.—Average Monthly Separation Rates of Workers on Relief, Regular Closings, by Age, Experience Status, and Employment Status, 13 Cities, October—December 1935

Age and experience status	Average monthly relief load	Average number separated monthly	Separation rate					Employment status at regular closing	Percent distribution			
			Total	Continuously employed	Secured employment	Employment unknown	Unemployed	Total	Continuously employed	Secured employment	Employment unknown	Unemployed
ALL WORKERS												
Total	437,500	21,010	4.8	0.5	2.4	0.3	1.6	100.0	11.0	49.9	5.1	34.0
—19 years	48,000	2,338	4.9	0.6	0.7	0.1	3.5	100.0	11.1	14.7	2.8	71.4
20—24 years	54,200	2,944	5.4	0.8	2.1	0.2	2.3	100.0	15.5	38.7	4.1	41.7
25—34 years	89,200	5,730	6.4	0.7	3.8	0.3	1.6	100.0	10.2	59.9	4.6	25.3
35—44 years	110,200	5,465	5.0	0.5	3.0	0.3	1.2	100.0	9.7	60.5	5.1	24.7
45—54 years	92,700	3,349	3.6	0.4	1.9	0.3	1.0	100.0	11.3	51.9	7.8	29.0
55—64 years	43,200	1,184	2.7	0.2	1.2	0.2	1.1	100.0	8.3	45.0	6.5	40.2
EXPERIENCED WORKERS												
Total	370,900	18,537	5.0	0.6	2.7	0.3	1.4	100.0	12.4	54.7	5.4	27.5
—19 years	12,900	842	6.5	2.0	1.3	0.4	2.8	100.0	30.8	20.6	5.6	43.0
20—24 years	39,200	2,399	6.1	1.1	2.7	0.3	2.0	100.0	19.0	43.4	4.2	33.4
25—34 years	83,500	5,547	6.7	0.7	4.1	0.3	1.6	100.0	10.5	61.4	4.3	23.8
35—44 years	104,900	5,319	5.1	0.5	3.1	0.3	1.2	100.0	10.0	61.6	5.2	23.2
45—54 years	89,200	3,276	3.7	0.4	2.0	0.3	1.0	100.0	11.6	52.3	7.9	28.2
55—64 years	41,800	1,154	2.8	0.2	1.3	0.2	1.1	100.0	8.5	44.7	6.5	40.3
INEXPERIENCED WORKERS												
Total	66,600	2,473	3.7	—	0.5	0.1	3.1	100.0	—	14.8	2.7	82.5
—19 years	35,100	1,496	4.3	—	0.5	0.1	3.7	100.0	—	11.4	1.2	87.4
20—24 years	15,000	545	3.6	—	0.6	0.1	2.9	100.0	—	17.9	3.5	78.6
25—34 years	5,700	183	3.2	—	0.4	0.5	2.3	100.0	—	13.3	13.8	72.9
35—44 years	5,900	146	2.5	—	0.5	0.1	1.9	100.0	—	20.1	3.2	76.7
45—54 years	3,500	73	2.1	—	0.7	—	1.4	100.0	—	35.5	—	64.5
55—64 years	1,400	30	2.1	—	1.2	0.1	0.8	100.0	—	57.8	4.4	37.8

Table 56.—Average Monthly Separation Rates of Workers on Relief, Regular Closings, by Race, Sex, Experience Status, and Employment Status, 13 Cities, October—December 1935

Race, sex, and experience status	Average monthly relief load	Average number separated monthly	Separation rate					Employment status at regular closing Percent distribution				
			Total	Continuously employed	Secured employment	Employment unknown	Unemployed	Total	Continuously employed	Secured employment	Employment unknown	Unemployed
ALL WORKERS												
Total[1]	437,500	21,010	4.8	0.5	2.4	0.3	1.6	100.0	11.0	49.9	5.1	34.0
White	319,200	16,894	5.3	0.6	2.8	0.3	1.6	100.0	10.8	53.7	5.8	29.7
Negro	112,000	3,905	3.5	0.4	1.2	0.1	1.8	100.0	11.9	33.6	2.0	52.5
Male	299,900	15,521	5.2	0.5	3.1	0.3	1.3	100.0	8.8	60.4	5.4	25.4
White	230,700	13,295	5.8	0.5	3.6	0.3	1.4	100.0	8.6	61.4	5.9	24.1
Negro	64,100	2,060	3.2	0.3	1.7	0.1	1.1	100.0	10.2	53.7	2.2	33.9
Female	137,600	5,489	4.0	0.7	0.8	0.2	2.3	100.0	17.2	20.4	4.1	58.3
White	88,500	3,599	4.1	0.8	1.0	0.2	2.1	100.0	18.8	25.1	5.3	50.8
Negro	47,900	1,845	3.8	0.5	0.4	0.1	2.8	100.0	13.8	11.3	1.8	73.1
EXPERIENCED WORKERS												
Total	370,900	18,537	5.0	0.6	2.7	0.3	1.4	100.0	12.4	54.7	5.4	27.5
White	264,700	14,754	5.6	0.7	3.3	0.4	1.2	100.0	12.3	59.2	6.2	22.3
Negro	100,900	3,604	3.6	0.5	1.3	0.1	1.7	100.0	12.9	36.0	1.8	49.3
Male	273,500	14,356	5.3	0.5	3.4	0.3	1.1	100.0	9.5	64.1	5.8	20.6
White	208,300	12,244	5.9	0.5	3.9	0.4	1.1	100.0	9.3	65.5	6.3	18.9
Negro	60,500	1,965	3.2	0.3	1.8	0.1	1.0	100.0	10.7	55.7	2.3	31.3
Female	97,400	4,181	4.3	1.0	0.9	0.2	2.2	100.0	22.6	22.0	4.0	51.4
White	56,400	2,510	4.5	1.2	1.3	0.3	1.7	100.0	27.0	28.4	5.8	38.8
Negro	40,400	1,639	4.0	0.6	0.5	*	2.9	100.0	15.6	12.3	1.2	70.9
INEXPERIENCED WORKERS												
Total	66,600	2,473	3.7	—	0.5	0.1	3.1	100.0	—	14.8	2.7	82.5
White	54,500	2,140	3.9	—	0.6	0.1	3.2	100.0	—	16.1	2.6	81.3
Negro	11,100	301	2.7	—	0.2	0.1	2.4	100.0	—	5.6	4.3	90.1

Male -----------	26,400	1,165	4.4	—	0.6	*	3.8	100.0	—	14.2	0.9	84.9
White ----------	22,400	1,051	4.7	—	0.7	*	4.0	100.0	—	14.4	1.0	84.6
Negro ----------	3,600	95	2.7	—	0.3	—	2.4	100.0	—	17.6	—	88.4
Female ---------	40,200	1,308	3.2	—	0.5	0.1	2.6	100.0	—	15.3	4.4	80.3
White ----------	32,100	1,089	3.4	—	0.6	0.1	2.7	100.0	—	17.7	4.1	78.2
Negro ----------	7,500	206	2.8	—	0.1	0.2	2.5	100.0	—	2.9	6.3	90.8

*Less than 0.05 percent.

¹All totals and subtotals include workers of "other" races.

Table 57.—Average Monthly Separation Rates of Workers on Relief, Regular Closings, by Usual Occupational Group, 13 Cities, October—December 1935

Usual occupational group	Average monthly relief load	Average number separated monthly	Employment status at regular closing									
			Separation rate					Percent distribution				
			Total	Continuously employed	Secured employment	Employment unknown	Unemployed	Total	Continuously employed	Secured employment	Employment unknown	Unemployed
Total workers----	370,900	18,587	5.0	0.6	2.7	0.3	1.4	100.0	12.4	54.7	5.4	27.5
White-collar-------	66,200	2,690	3.9	0.6	1.8	0.3	1.2	100.0	15.2	46.1	7.6	31.1
Skilled-----------	51,500	2,699	5.2	0.4	3.5	0.3	1.0	100.0	7.1	68.1	5.8	19.0
Semiskilled-------	119,900	6,841	5.7	0.7	3.6	0.2	1.2	100.0	12.9	61.6	3.8	21.7
Unskilled---------	131,900	6,307	4.8	0.6	2.2	0.3	1.7	100.0	13.0	45.0	6.0	36.0

Table 58.—Average Monthly Relief Load of Inexperienced Workers, by Sex and Age, 13 Cities, October—December 1935

Sex	Inexperienced workers		Age in years					
	Number	Percent	16—19	20—24	25—34	35—44	45—54	55—64
Total_____	66,600	100.0	52.6	22.6	8.6	8.8	5.2	2.2
Male_____	26,400	39.6	25.3	13.1	0.6	0.3	0.2	0.1
Female_____	40,200	60.4	27.3	9.5	8.0	8.5	5.0	2.1

Table 59.—Average Monthly Separation Rates of Experienced Workers[1] on Relief, by Duration of Unemployment, 13 Cities, October—December 1935

Duration of unemployment	Experienced workers on relief		Average monthly separation rate (percent)			
	Average monthly number	Percent distribution	Total	Secured employment	Employment unknown	Unemployed
Total_____	347,800	100.0	4.7	2.9	0.3	1.5
Less than 6 months_____	44,700	12.9	15.7	12.4	0.8	2.5
6.0—11.9 months_____	44,800	12.9	5.9	3.7	0.4	1.8
12.0—17.9 months_____	46,500	13.4	3.9	1.9	0.4	1.6
18.0—23.9 months_____	37,700	10.8	3.1	1.5	0.1	1.5
24.0—29.9 months_____	33,100	9.5	2.6	1.1	0.1	1.4
30.0—35.9 months_____	20,600	5.9	2.5	0.9	0.2	1.4
36.0—41.9 months_____	21,900	6.3	2.7	1.2	0.1	1.4
42.0—47.9 months_____	19,200	5.5	2.4	1.1	0.2	1.1
48.0—59.9 months_____	37,900	10.9	1.6	0.7	0.1	0.8
60.0—71.9 months_____	25,700	7.4	1.5	0.7	0.1	0.7
72.0—95.9 months_____	13,800	4.0	1.5	0.6	0.1	0.8
96.0—119.9 months_____	1,900	0.5	2.2	0.9	0.1	1.2

[1]Excludes those continuously employed for at least 4 weeks prior to closing.

Table 60.—Average Monthly Separation Rates of Experienced Workers[1] on Relief, by Duration of Unemployment, Age, Sex, and Race, 13 Cities, October—December 1935

Duration of unemployment	All workers	Age in years						Sex		Race[2]					
										White			Negro		
		16—19	20—24	25—34	35—44	45—54	55—64	Male	Female	Total	Male	Female	Total	Male	Female
Total[3]	4.7	6.6	5.8	6.2	4.8	3.4	2.6	4.9	4.0	5.2	5.5	4.0	3.4	2.9	4.1
3.0—3.9 months	16.2	5.0	15.8	23.1	17.9	11.8	11.3	18.3	8.3	18.1	20.0	9.2	9.6	11.1	6.7
4.0—4.9 months	13.9	10.0	13.7	17.9	13.4	12.2	10.0	14.7	10.6	15.0	15.4	12.5	10.9	11.8	8.8
5.0—5.9 months	10.5	7.0	9.9	12.2	12.5	7.7	7.0	11.7	6.0	11.3	12.2	6.9	8.0	9.7	4.6
6.0—8.9 months	7.0	7.5	7.7	8.8	7.2	4.8	4.2	7.1	6.4	7.4	7.8	6.0	5.5	4.4	7.4
9.0—11.9 months	4.6	10.2	5.3	5.0	3.9	3.7	5.6	4.8	4.0	5.2	5.6	3.8	3.0	2.4	4.4
12.0—14.9 months	4.0	6.8	5.4	4.7	3.5	3.6	2.5	4.0	4.0	4.6	4.9	3.9	2.5	1.8	3.9
15.0—17.9 months	3.7	5.5	5.8	3.7	3.5	3.4	2.7	3.6	4.0	4.1	4.0	4.5	3.0	2.5	3.7
18.0—20.9 months	3.0	4.9	3.0	3.9	2.8	2.9	1.3	2.9	3.3	2.7	2.9	2.0	3.6	2.7	4.8
21.0—23.9 months	3.1	4.6	3.9	4.0	3.0	2.5	1.8	3.0	3.3	3.3	3.5	2.7	2.8	2.1	4.0
24.0—29.9 months	2.6	5.1	3.5	3.1	2.4	2.2	1.8	2.2	3.6	2.3	2.3	2.4	3.2	1.9	4.9
30.0—35.9 months	2.5	2.3	4.0	3.2	2.3	1.7	2.2	2.3	2.9	2.4	2.4	2.1	2.7	1.8	3.8
36.0—41.9 months	2.7	3.2	4.2	2.9	3.0	2.0	2.2	2.3	4.3	2.9	2.7	4.4	2.2	1.0	4.2
42.0—47.9 months	2.4	9.1	2.8	2.8	2.5	2.2	1.4	2.3	2.6	2.5	2.6	2.1	2.2	1.6	3.5
48.0—59.9 months	1.6	4.6	2.1	2.0	1.9	1.1	1.3	1.6	2.0	1.8	1.7	2.5	1.1	1.0	1.4
60.0—71.9 months	1.5	1.0	2.1	3.0	1.1	1.0	1.1	1.4	1.7	1.6	1.5	2.2	1.1	1.2	1.0
72.0—95.9 months	1.5	—	2.5	2.0	1.6	1.0	1.5	1.3	2.3	1.7	1.5	2.6	1.1	0.6	1.9
96.0—119.9 months	2.2	—	—	4.3	2.6	0.7	1.0	1.9	2.4	3.3	2.4	4.7	0.7	0.9	0.6

[1]Excludes those continuously employed for at least 4 weeks prior to closing.
[2]"Other" races not shown because of relatively small numbers involved.
[3]Based upon data for workers with durations from 1 day to 119.9 months, although the separate rates for durations shorter than 3.0 months are not shown in the table.

Table 61.—Average Monthly Reemployment Rates of Experienced Workers[1] on Relief, by Duration of Unemployment and Age, 13 Cities, October—December 1935

Duration of unemployment	Total	Age in years					
		16—19	20—24	25—34	35—44	45—54	55—64
Total[2]_____	2.9	2.0	3.1	4.3	3.3	2.0	1.3

Average reemployment rates derived from original data

Duration of unemployment	Total	16—19	20—24	25—34	35—44	45—54	55—64
3.0—3.9 months_____	13.0	1.4	11.6	19.3	15.3	9.1	8.1
4.0—4.9 months_____	11.1	4.1	10.4	14.8	11.2	9.3	8.1
5.0—5.9 months_____	8.3	4.2	7.0	9.7	10.7	5.9	5.1
6.0—8.9 months_____	4.6	2.7	4.4	6.6	5.0	3.0	2.4
9.0—11.9 months_____	2.6	2.4	2.7	3.1	2.2	2.2	3.3
12.0—14.9 months_____	1.9	0.7	2.0	2.6	2.1	1.6	1.0
15.0—17.9 months_____	1.9	1.5	2.3	2.2	2.0	2.0	1.0
18.0—20.9 months_____	1.4	1.2	1.1	1.7	1.5	1.3	0.6
21.0—23.9 months_____	1.5	2.3	1.9	2.2	1.5	1.0	0.6
24.0—29.9 months_____	1.1	0.5	1.0	1.3	1.2	0.9	0.5
30.0—35.9 months_____	0.9	0.2	1.1	1.2	0.8	0.7	1.1
36.0—41.9 months_____	1.2	0.1	1.4	1.1	1.8	1.1	0.5
42.0—47.9 months_____	1.1	2.0	0.7	1.8	1.2	0.8	0.4
48.0—59.9 months_____	0.7	2.3	0.5	0.9	1.0	0.5	0.3
60.0—71.9 months_____	0.7	—	0.5	1.5	0.6	0.5	0.4
72.0—95.9 months_____	0.6	—	0.8	1.1	0.6	0.3	0.4
96.0—119.9 months_____	0.9	—	—	2.7	0.7	0.1	—

Generalization of average reemployment rates[3]

Duration of unemployment	Total	16—19	20—24	25—34	35—44	45—54	55—64
3.0—3.9 months_____	13.7	3.2	11.5	20.0	15.2	9.7	9.4
4.0—4.9 months_____	9.6	2.8	8.6	13.4	10.6	7.1	6.4
5.0—5.9 months_____	7.3	2.5	6.8	9.8	7.9	5.5	4.8
6.0—8.9 months_____	4.8	2.1	4.8	6.2	5.2	3.8	3.0
9.0—11.9 months_____	3.1	1.7	3.3	3.8	3.3	2.6	1.9
12.0—14.9 months_____	2.3	1.5	2.5	2.8	2.5	1.9	1.4
15.0—17.9 months_____	1.8	1.3	2.0	2.2	2.0	1.6	1.1
18.0—20.9 months_____	1.6	1.1	1.7	1.9	1.6	1.3	0.9
21.0—23.9 months_____	1.4	1.0	1.4	1.6	1.4	1.1	0.7
24.0—29.9 months_____	1.2	0.9	1.2	1.4	1.2	1.0	0.6
30.0—35.9 months_____	1.0	0.7	1.0	1.3	1.1	0.8	0.5
36.0—41.9 months_____	0.9	0.6	0.8	1.2	1.0	0.7	0.5
42.0—47.9 months_____	0.8	0.5	0.7	1.2	0.9	0.7	0.4
48.0—59.9 months_____	0.8	0.4	0.6	1.3	0.9	0.6	0.4
60.0—71.9 months_____	0.8	—	0.5	1.4	0.9	0.6	0.4

[1] Excludes those continuously employed for at least 4 weeks prior to closing.

[2] Based upon data for workers with durations from 1 day to 119.9 months, although the separate rates for durations shorter than 3.0 months are not shown in the table.

[3] Computed from the midpoints of the duration intervals.

Table 62.—Duration of Unemployment of Experienced Workers on Relief,[1] by Age, Sex, Race, and Usual Occupational Group, 13 Cities, September—November 1935

Age, sex, race, and usual occupational group	Experienced workers		Duration of unemployment[2]					Average[3] unemployment in months
	Number	Percent	Less than 1 year	1 year	2 years	3 years	4—9 years	
Total---------------	347,800	100.0	25.7	24.2	15.5	11.8	22.8	24.0
AGE								
16—19 years-------------	8,900	100.0	50.7	30.8	13.4	3.2	1.9	11.7
20—24 years-------------	33,500	100.0	34.8	25.6	15.9	7.8	15.9	18.9
25—34 years-------------	79,700	100.0	28.6	25.1	16.2	11.7	18.4	21.9
35—44 years-------------	99,500	100.0	25.2	24.7	16.2	11.8	22.1	24.1
45—54 years-------------	85,500	100.0	21.9	23.0	14.1	13.5	27.5	27.6
55—64 years-------------	40,900	100.0	16.8	21.1	15.1	13.7	33.3	33.0
SEX								
Male--------------------	266,800	100.0	25.8	23.2	14.3	12.4	24.3	24.7
Female------------------	81,000	100.0	25.7	27.3	19.4	10.0	17.6	22.8
RACE								
White-------------------	248,600	100.0	27.3	22.5	14.5	11.8	23.9	24.1
Negro-------------------	94,000	100.0	21.8	28.5	18.1	11.7	19.9	23.9
Other-------------------	5,200	100.0	22.7	28.9	11.9	13.1	23.4	22.5
USUAL OCCUPATIONAL GROUP								
White-collar-------------	62,100	100.0	27.0	24.7	16.1	13.5	18.7	23.4
Skilled------------------	50,800	100.0	23.7	22.1	13.4	11.9	28.9	28.0
Semiskilled--------------	111,600	100.0	30.2	22.0	15.4	11.2	21.2	23.1
Unskilled----------------	123,300	100.0	25.2	25.1	15.3	11.6	22.8	24.1

[1]Excludes those employed throughout the last 4 weeks on relief.

[2]Duration of unemployment is reported in full years. For example, the designation 1 year is more correctly designated as 12.0 through 23.9 months.

[3]Median.

Table 63.—Average Monthly Reemployment Rates of Experienced Workers[1] on Relief, by Duration of Unemployment, Race, and Sex, 13 Cities, October—December 1935

Duration of unemployment	All races[2]			White			Negro		
	Total	Male	Female	Total	Male	Female	Total	Male	Female
Total[3]	2.9	3.5	1.1	3.5	4.0	1.6	1.4	1.8	0.6
Average reemployment rates derived from original data									
3.0—3.9 months	13.0	15.4	4.0	14.7	16.8	5.0	7.1	9.7	2.2
4.0—4.9 months	11.1	12.6	4.8	12.3	13.3	6.3	7.7	9.7	2.9
5.0—5.9 months	8.3	9.9	2.1	9.0	10.2	3.0	6.2	8.9	0.9
6.0—8.9 months	4.6	5.4	1.9	5.2	6.0	2.3	2.3	3.0	1.1
9.0—11.9 months	2.6	3.0	1.4	3.1	3.5	1.7	1.2	1.4	0.9
12.0—14.9 months	1.9	2.3	0.9	2.4	2.8	1.0	0.8	1.0	0.7
15.0—17.9 months	1.9	2.2	1.0	2.3	2.4	1.8	1.1	1.6	0.4
18.0—20.9 months	1.4	1.6	0.7	1.5	1.7	0.8	1.0	1.2	0.6
21.0—23.9 months	1.5	1.7	0.8	2.0	2.3	1.2	0.6	0.8	0.4
24.0—29.9 months	1.1	1.3	0.6	1.2	1.4	0.6	0.7	0.8	0.6
30.0—35.9 months	0.9	1.1	0.5	1.1	1.2	0.6	0.4	0.5	0.4
36.0—41.9 months	1.2	1.3	0.9	1.6	1.7	1.8	0.3	0.4	0.2
42.0—47.9 months	1.1	1.2	0.4	1.3	1.4	0.6	0.6	0.7	0.2
48.0—59.9 months	0.7	0.8	0.3	0.8	0.8	0.4	0.4	0.4	0.3
60.0—71.9 months	0.7	0.7	0.3	0.8	0.8	0.3	0.4	0.5	0.2
72.0—95.9 months	0.6	0.5	0.8	0.7	0.6	1.1	0.2	0.1	0.5
96.0—119.9 months	0.9	0.3	1.4	1.5	0.5	3.0	0.1	0.1	—
Generalization of average reemployment rates[4]									
3.0—3.9 months	13.7	15.8	4.2	14.8	16.6	5.2	9.2	12.4	2.3
4.0—4.9 months	9.6	11.2	3.3	10.7	12.0	4.2	6.1	8.0	1.8
5.0—5.9 months	7.3	8.5	2.7	8.2	9.3	3.5	4.4	5.7	1.5
6.0—8.9 months	4.8	5.7	2.0	5.6	6.3	2.6	2.7	3.5	1.1
9.0—11.9 months	3.1	3.7	1.5	3.7	4.2	1.9	1.6	2.1	0.8
12.0—14.9 months	2.3	2.7	1.1	2.8	3.1	1.5	1.2	1.4	0.6
15.0—17.9 months	1.8	2.2	1.0	2.3	2.5	1.3	0.9	1.1	0.5
18.0—20.9 months	1.6	1.8	0.8	1.9	2.1	1.1	0.7	0.9	0.5
21.0—23.9 months	1.4	1.6	0.7	1.7	1.8	1.1	0.6	0.8	0.4
24.0—29.9 months	1.2	1.3	0.6	1.4	1.6	0.8	0.5	0.7	0.4
30.0—35.9 months	1.0	1.1	0.5	1.2	1.3	0.7	0.5	0.6	0.3
36.0—41.9 months	0.9	1.0	0.5	1.0	1.2	0.6	0.4	0.5	0.3
42.0—47.9 months	0.8	0.9	0.4	1.0	1.1	0.6	0.4	0.5	0.3
48.0—59.9 months	0.8	0.9	0.4	0.9	1.0	0.5	0.4	0.5	0.2
60.0—71.9 months	0.8	0.9	0.3	0.9	1.0	0.4	0.4	0.5	0.2

[1]Excludes those continuously employed for the last 4 weeks prior to closing.
[2]Includes "other" races amounting to less than 2 percent of all workers on relief.
[3]Based upon data for workers with durations from 1 day to 119.9 months, although the separate rates for durations shorter than 3.0 months are not shown in the table.
[4]Computed from the midpoints of the duration intervals.

Table 64.—Average Monthly Reemployment Rates of Experienced Workers[1] on Relief, by Usual Occupational Group, 13 Cities, October—December 1935

Usual occupational group	Workers on relief	Workers obtaining employment	Reemployment rate (percent)
Total	347,800	10,129	2.9
White-collar	62,100	1,240	2.0
Skilled	50,800	1,837	3.6
Semiskilled	111,600	4,218	3.8
Unskilled	123,300	2,834	2.3

[1]Excludes those employed throughout the last 4 weeks on relief.

Table 65.—Average Monthly Reemployment Rates of Experienced Workers[1] on Relief, by Duration of Unemployment and Usual Occupational Group, 13 Cities, October—December 1935

Duration of unemployment	Total	Usual occupational group			
		White-collar	Skilled	Semi-skilled	Unskilled
Total[2] -------------------------	2.9	2.0	3.6	3.8	2.3
Average reemployment rates derived from original data					
2.2—4.0 months -------------------	15.4	6.6	15.4	22.1	14.2
4.1—6.1 months -------------------	9.1	4.0	10.5	11.7	7.3
6.2—12.1 months ------------------	3.5	3.1	4.9	3.8	2.8
12.2—24.1 months -----------------	1.8	1.7	2.5	1.9	1.5
24.2—36.1 months -----------------	1.0	1.1	1.7	0.8	0.9
36.2—48.1 months -----------------	1.1	1.2	2.5	0.9	0.7
48.2—120 months ------------------	0.6	0.6	0.8	0.6	0.5
Generalization of average reemployment rates[3]					
3.0—3.9 months -------------------	13.7	5.7	13.3	18.6	11.6
4.0—4.9 months -------------------	9.6	4.8	10.6	12.6	8.3
5.0—5.9 months -------------------	7.3	4.2	8.8	9.7	6.3
6.0—8.9 months -------------------	4.8	3.3	6.7	5.8	4.2
9.0—11.9 months ------------------	3.1	2.6	5.0	3.6	2.7
12.0—14.9 months -----------------	2.3	2.2	4.0	2.6	2.0
15.0—17.9 months -----------------	1.8	1.9	3.3	2.0	1.6
18.0—20.9 months -----------------	1.6	1.7	2.9	1.6	1.3
21.0—23.9 months -----------------	1.4	1.5	2.6	1.4	1.2
24.0—29.9 months -----------------	1.2	1.4	2.2	1.1	1.0
30.0—35.9 months -----------------	1.0	1.2	1.9	0.9	0.8
36.0—41.9 months -----------------	0.9	1.1	1.7	0.8	0.7
42.0—47.9 months -----------------	0.8	1.0	1.5	0.7	0.6
48.0—59.9 months -----------------	0.8	0.9	1.3	0.7	0.6
60.0—71.9 months -----------------	0.8	0.8	1.1	0.6	0.5

[1]Excludes those continuously employed for at least 4 weeks prior to closing.

[2]Based upon the data for workers with durations from 1 day to 120 months, although the separate rates for durations shorter than 2.2 months are not shown in the table.

[3]Derived from original data for the period from 3.0 to 119.9 months and based upon the midpoints of the duration intervals. For workers unemployed 3.0 months the rates are: white-collar, 6.4; skilled, 15.3; semiskilled, 23.8; and unskilled, 14.3.

Table 66.—Number of Persons Unemployed and Number of Cases Receiving Relief or Wage Assistance, 1933—1936[1]

Number of persons unemployed	Number of cases receiving relief or wage assistance
1933	**1933**
High (March) -------------------------- 13,857,000	High (March) -------------------------- 5,080,000
Low (October) ------------------------- 10,055,000	Low (September) ----------------------- 3,405,000
Average ------------------------------- 12,006,000	Average ------------------------------- 4,213,000
1934	**1934**
High (January) ------------------------ 11,543,000	High (December) ----------------------- 5,112,000
Low (June) ---------------------------- 9,327,000	Low (June) --------------------------- 4,269,000
Average ------------------------------- 10,090,000	Average ------------------------------- 4,704,000
1935	**1935**
High (January) ------------------------ 10,633,000	High (January) ------------------------ 5,316,000
Low (October) ------------------------- 8,230,000	Low (September) ----------------------- 4,149,000
Average ------------------------------- 9,239,000	Average ------------------------------- 4,677,000
1936	**1936**
High (January) ------------------------ 9,882,000	High (February) ----------------------- 4,950,000
Low (October) ------------------------- 6,588,000	Low (November) ----------------------- 3,627,000
Average ------------------------------- 7,948,000	Average ------------------------------- 4,116,000

[1]Revised series of unemployment estimates made by Robert R. Nathan. See *Selected Current Statistics,* Social Security Board, Vol. 2, No. 3, Washington, D. C., September 1937, p. 58. The relief and wage assistance series is an extension and revision of the one appearing in the Division of Research, Statistics, and Records, *Monthly Report of the Federal Emergency Relief Administration, June 1 Through June 30, 1936.* Federal Emergency Relief Administration, Washington, D. C., 1937, p. 2.

Table 67.—Proportion of Relief Cases Closed During 1935 Because of Works Program Employment, by Race, Employability, and Size of Case, 13 Cities

Race, employability, and size of case	Cases on relief July 1935	Cases closed by Works Program employment	
		Number	Percent of July 1935 load
Total	345,500	151,821	43.9
RACE			
White	251,200	110,173	43.9
Negro	88,500	39,313	44.4
Other	5,800	2,335	40.3
EMPLOYABILITY[1]			
Cases with workers	307,700	148,524	48.3
Cases without workers	37,800	3,297	8.7
SIZE OF CASE			
1 person	77,400	31,372	40.5
2 persons	73,900	34,899	47.2
3 persons	59,800	26,429	44.2
4 persons	49,400	22,283	45.1
5 persons	35,400	14,987	42.3
6 persons	20,400	9,194	45.1
7 persons	12,500	5,790	46.3
8 persons	7,400	3,012	40.7
9 persons	4,500	1,913	42.5
10 persons or more	4,800	1,942	40.5

[1]In this study a worker has been defined as any person 16 to 64 years of age, inclusive, who is either working or seeking work. Since there is no definite upper age limit on the Works Program, it was possible for some relief cases that were technically without "workers" to be transferred to the Program.

Table 68.—Workers Transferred From Relief to the Works Program, by Race, Sex, and Experience Status, 13 Cities, July—December 1935

Race, sex, and experience status	Workers on relief July 1935	Workers in cases transferred to Works Program as percent of July load		
		Total	Employed on Works Program	Not employed on Works Program
Total[1]	447,300	46.0	33.3	12.7
RACE AND SEX				
White	326,500	45.5	33.0	12.5
Male	236,800	49.8	41.6	8.2
Female	89,700	34.1	10.2	23.9
Negro	114,100	47.5	34.1	13.4
Male	65,400	56.4	51.5	4.9
Female	48,700	35.6	10.8	24.8
SEX				
Male	307,600	51.2	43.7	7.5
Female	139,700	34.6	10.4	24.2
EXPERIENCE STATUS				
Inexperienced	69,300	42.3	11.6	30.7
Experienced	378,000	46.7	37.3	9.4
White-collar	68,800	36.0	27.9	8.1
Skilled	53,100	43.0	40.6	2.4
Semiskilled	119,500	42.6	32.2	10.4
Unskilled	136,600	57.1	45.1	12.0
Manual	65,700	74.2	68.1	6.1
Domestic and personal service	70,900	41.2	23.7	17.5

[1]Total includes "other" races.

Table 69.—Relief Income of Cases on Relief Throughout May 1935 With No Private-Employment Income, 13 Cities

[A 4-percent sample of the May 1935 case load[1]]

Relief income (nearest dollar)	Size of case								
	Total	1 person	2 persons	3 persons	4 persons	5 persons	6 persons	7 persons	8 persons or more
Total cases _____	7,428	1,836	1,615	1,257	1,033	735	404	244	304
Cases not reporting _____	20	3	5	1	4	1	5	1	—
Cases reporting: Number _____	7,408	1,833	1,610	1,256	1,029	734	399	243	304
Percent _____	100.0	100.0	100.0	100.0	100.0	100.0	100.0	100.0	100.0
$4 or less _____	2.5	7.6	2.0	0.4	0.4	0.1	1.0	—	—
$5—$9 _____	13.8	41.0	10.0	2.9	4.6	3.0	0.7	0.4	0.7
$10—$14 _____	11.2	20.2	15.0	8.8	6.2	2.5	4.8	1.2	1.2
$15—$19 _____	12.0	10.0	27.5	11.1	5.2	5.0	4.5	0.8	4.3
$20—$24 _____	11.3	8.4	13.6	23.9	9.4	4.9	6.3	2.5	0.7
$25—$29 _____	12.0	5.7	9.8	18.6	27.5	10.1	3.5	4.5	2.3
$30—$34 _____	8.5	4.9	8.7	8.7	12.1	16.1	6.5	6.2	3.3
$35—$39 _____	6.1	1.1	4.4	6.4	6.8	16.8	11.8	8.6	5.3
$40—$44 _____	4.8	0.3	2.4	6.2	6.0	10.6	15.3	9.9	3.3
$45—$49 _____	4.1	0.2	2.5	4.0	6.0	7.1	10.0	16.9	4.9
$50—$54 _____	3.2	0.2	1.3	2.6	3.9	5.9	9.0	15.2	7.6
$55—$59 _____	2.7	0.1	1.4	1.3	3.7	4.4	7.3	9.5	12.8
$60—$69 _____	3.5	0.1	0.6	2.9	3.7	6.1	8.8	11.1	21.7
$70—$79 _____	2.2	0.1	0.4	1.6	2.5	3.4	6.3	7.0	13.5
$80—$89 _____	1.0	—	0.1	0.4	1.5	1.4	1.8	2.5	9.2
$90—$99 _____	0.6	—	0.1	0.2	0.4	2.0	1.7	2.1	3.9
$100—$109 _____	0.2	—	0.2	—	—	0.3	0.7	0.4	2.0
$110—$119 _____	0.1	0.1	—	—	—	0.1	—	0.4	0.7
$120—$129 _____	0.1	—	—	—	0.1	0.1	—	0.8	1.3
$130—$139 _____	*	—	—	—	—	0.1	—	—	—
$140—$149 _____	*	—	—	—	—	—	—	—	0.3
$150 or more _____	0.1	—	—	—	—	—	—	—	1.0
Average[2] relief income ____	$24.10	$9.80	$18.70	$25.30	$28.90	$37.00	$43.10	$49.20	$61.20

*Less than 0.05 percent.

[1]The sample of the May 1935 case load taken varied from 1 percent in Chicago and 4 percent in Detroit and St. Louis to approximately 10 percent in the smaller cities. The sample yielded 14,174 cases or about 4 percent of the May 1935 case load. In computing the aggregate for 13 cities, each city was weighted according to its May 1935 case load and the aggregate reduced arbitrarily to 10,000 cases. Of this total 7,428 cases were reported on relief throughout May 1935 and without private-employment income. For further details see Carmichael, F. L. and Payne, Stanley L., The 1935 Relief Population in 13 Cities: A Cross-Section, Research Bulletin Series I, No. 23, Division of Social Research, Works Progress Administration, Washington, D. C., December 31, 1936.

[2]Median.

Table 70.—Distribution of Monthly Works Program Wage Rates of Closed Relief Cases, by Amount of Relief Granted Same Cases During Last 30 Days on Relief, 13 Cities, October—December 1935

[Distribution for every 1,000 cases]

Monthly Works Program wage rate	Total	Monthly relief grant											Average relief grant	
		Less than $10	$10—$19	$20—$29	$30—$39	$40—$49	$50—$59	$60—$69	$70—$79	$80—$89	$90—$99	$100 or more	Median	Mean
Total	1,000	58	232	253	180	122	76	39	22	8	5	5	$28	$31
$30—$39	52	14	15	16	6	1	—	—	—	—	—	—	18	18
$40—$49	86	2	20	20	18	13	8	3	2	—	—	—	30	32
$50—$59	627	37	150	157	115	75	47	22	13	5	3	3	27	31
$60—$69	172	3	38	47	27	22	15	9	5	3	1	2	29	34
$70—$79	13	—	1	2	3	2	2	1	1	—	1	—	39	43
$80—$89	33	1	4	7	7	7	3	3	1	—	—	—	34	37
$90—$99	14	1	3	3	3	2	1	1	—	—	—	—	31	35
$100 or more	3	—	1	1	1	—	—	—	—	—	—	—	30	37
AVERAGE WORKS PROGRAM WAGE RATE														
Median	$55	$53	$55	$55	$55	$56	$56	$57	$57	$57	$58	$59		
Mean	56	51	55	56	57	58	58	59	59	60	61	62		

Note.—Figures in boldface indicate Works Program wage rates and relief grants in same class intervals; items above the figures in boldface include all cases in which Works Program rates exceed relief grants; items below the figures in boldface include all cases in which relief grants exceed Works Program wage rates.

Table 71.—Comparison of Monthly Works Program Wage Rates With Relief Grants to the Same Cases During Last 30 Days on Relief, Works Program Closings, by Race and Family Status, 13 Cities, October—December 1935

Race and family status	Total cases		Comparison of wage rates and relief grants		
	Number	Percent	Wage rates higher than relief grants	Wage rates lower than relief grants	Wage rates same as relief grants[1]
ALL CASES					
Total	136,300	100.0	85.2	7.2	7.6
White	98,500	100.0	84.6	7.6	7.8
Negro	35,600	100.0	87.2	5.5	7.3
Other	2,200	100.0	79.4	14.1	6.5
FAMILY CASES					
Total	107,300	100.0	81.4	9.1	9.5
White	76,900	100.0	80.5	9.7	9.8
Negro	28,800	100.0	84.4	6.8	8.8
Other	1,600	100.0	72.5	18.8	8.7
NONFAMILY CASES					
Total	29,000	100.0	99.3	0.2	0.5
White	21,600	100.0	99.3	0.3	0.4
Negro	6,800	100.0	99.1	*	0.9
Other	600	100.0	99.8	0.2	—

*Less than 0.05 percent.

[1]In same $10-class interval.

Table 72.—Differentials Between Monthly Works Program Wage Rates and Relief Grants to Same Cases During Last 30 Days on Relief, Works Program Closings, 13 Cities, October—December 1935

Differentials between Works Program wage rates and relief grants	Total[1]	Family	Nonfamily	White	Negro
Total: Number	136,322	107,277	29,045	98,549	35,583
Percent	100.0	100.0	100.0	100.0	100.0
Wage rates exceed relief grants	85.2	81.4	99.3	84.6	87.2
Wage rates and relief grants in same $10 interval	7.6	9.5	0.5	7.8	7.3
Relief grants exceed wage rates	7.2	9.1	0.2	7.6	5.5
Differentials[2]					
Wage rates exceed relief grants by:					
$60 a month or more	2.9	2.4	4.8	3.8	0.8
$50 a month	8.6	4.2	24.9	9.7	5.6
$40 a month	21.0	15.7	40.9	20.1	23.3
$30 a month	22.4	22.5	21.8	21.0	26.4
$20 a month	17.7	21.1	5.3	17.4	18.5
$10 a month	12.6	15.5	1.6	12.6	12.6
Wage rates and relief grants in same $10 interval	7.6	9.5	0.5	7.8	7.3
Relief grants exceed wage rates by:					
$10 a month	3.6	4.6	0.1	3.8	2.8
$20 a month	2.0	2.5	0.1	2.2	1.5
$30 a month	0.8	1.1	*	0.9	0.6
$40 a month	0.5	0.6	—	0.5	0.4
$50 a month or more	0.3	0.3	—	0.2	0.2

*Less than 0.05 percent.

[1]Includes "other" races.

[2]The data were first grouped in $10 intervals of relief grants and Works Program wage rates. The differentials shown are the differences between the midpoints of the relief and wage rate intervals. For example, cases with former relief grants ranging from $30 to $39 (midpoint $34.50) and Works Program wage rates ranging from $50 to $59 (midpoint $54.50) have been shown in the category *Works Program wage rates exceed relief grants by $20 a month.*

Table 73.—Monthly Private-Employment Wage Rates of Closed Relief Cases, by Amount of Relief Granted Same Cases During Last 30 Days on Relief, 13 Cities, October—December 1935

[Distribution for every 1,000 cases]

Monthly private-employment wage rate	Total	Monthly relief grant											Average relief grant	
		Less than $10	$10—$19	$20—$29	$30—$39	$40—$49	$50—$59	$60—$69	$70—$79	$80—$89	$90—$99	$100 or more	Median	Mean
Total	1,000	73	172	216	195	142	93	55	30	12	7	5	$32	$34
Less than $10	8	1	2	3	1	—	—	1	—	—	—	—	22	23
$10—$19	15	2	5	4	3	1	—	—	—	—	—	—	20	21
$20—$29	21	4	6	6	2	1	1	1	—	—	—	—	21	23
$30—$39	27	4	9	8	3	1	1	1	—	—	—	—	20	23
$40—$49	43	5	11	11	8	5	2	—	1	—	—	—	24	26
$50—$59	78	9	18	20	15	8	5	3	—	—	—	—	25	27
$60—$69	115	11	22	29	23	16	8	3	2	1	—	—	28	30
$70—$79	97	7	19	23	19	12	8	5	3	1	—	—	30	33
$80—$89	121	7	18	28	23	18	11	8	4	2	1	1	33	36
$90—$99	87	6	12	17	16	15	9	6	3	2	1	—	35	37
$100—$109	110	6	15	22	23	15	13	7	5	2	1	1	34	38
$110—$119	51	2	9	9	12	8	5	3	1	1	1	—	34	36
$120—$129	56	3	8	8	12	9	7	3	3	1	1	1	36	38
$130—$139	81	3	10	13	17	17	9	6	3	1	1	1	38	40
$140—$149	24	1	3	4	5	4	4	2	1	—	—	—	38	40
$150—$159	20	1	2	4	4	3	3	2	1	—	—	—	39	40
$160—$169	11	—	1	2	2	2	2	1	1	—	—	—	40	42
$170 or more	35	1	2	5	7	7	5	3	2	1	1	1	42	44
AVERAGE PRIVATE-EMPLOYMENT RATE														
Median	$88	$69	$77	$81	$90	$96	$101	$100	$102	$104	$99	$116		
Mean	91	75	80	84	93	99	103	104	105	112	110	120		

Note.—Figures in boldface indicate private-employment wage rates and relief grants in same class interval; items above the figures in boldface include all cases in which private-employment rates exceed relief grants; items below the figures in boldface include all cases in which relief grants exceed private-employment wage rates.

Table 74.—Average[1] Works Program and Private-Employment Wage Rates Compared With Average[1] Relief Grants to Same Cases During Last 30 Days on Relief, by Race and Family Status, 13 Cities, Relief Cases Closed October—December 1935

Race	Works Program			Private employment		
	Total	Family	Nonfamily	Total	Family	Nonfamily
ALL RACES						
Wage rates	$55	$55	$56	$88	$89	$69
Relief grants	28	33	16	32	34	16
WHITE						
Wage rates	56	56	56	91	93	76
Relief grants	29	34	16	33	35	16
NEGRO						
Wage rates	54	54	54	70	73	39
Relief grants	25	28	15	26	27	13
OTHER						
Wage rates	56	53	63	77	78	75
Relief grants	26	33	18	27	28	21

[1]Median.

Table 75.—Differentials Between Monthly Private-Employment Wage Rates and Relief Grants to Same Cases During Last 30 Days on Relief, by Family Status and Race, 13 Cities, Relief Cases Closed October—December 1935

Differentials between private-employment wage rates and relief grants	Total[1]	Family	Nonfamily	White	Negro
Total: Number	31,297	28,479	2,818	26,526	4,473
Percent	100.0	100.0	100.0	100.0	100.0
Wage rates exceed relief grants	93.0	93.1	91.9	94.4	84.7
Wage rates and relief grants in same $10 interval	3.5	3.3	4.9	2.9	6.5
Relief grants exceed wage rates	3.5	3.6	3.2	2.7	8.8
Differentials[2]					
Wage rates exceed relief grants by:					
$100 a month or more	15.5	15.5	16.0	17.4	5.4
$90 a month	6.7	6.6	7.9	7.0	4.8
$80 a month	7.5	7.5	7.0	7.7	6.7
$70 a month	8.8	8.9	7.9	9.2	6.1
$60 a month	10.0	10.2	9.3	10.1	9.8
$50 a month	11.2	11.2	9.9	11.1	10.9
$40 a month	10.8	10.8	10.6	10.8	10.9
$30 a month	9.5	9.5	9.5	9.2	10.7
$20 a month	7.7	7.6	8.1	7.1	11.0
$10 a month	5.3	5.3	5.7	4.8	8.4
Wage rates and relief grants in same $10 interval	3.5	3.3	4.9	2.9	6.5
Relief grants exceed wage rates by:					
$10 a month	1.8	1.9	2.1	1.5	4.3
$20 a month	1.1	1.1	1.1	0.7	3.5
$30 a month	0.4	0.4	*	0.3	0.9
$40 a month	0.1	0.1	—	0.1	0.1
$50 a month or more	0.1	0.1	—	0.1	*

*Less than 0.05 percent.

[1]Includes "other" races.

[2]The data were first grouped in $10 intervals of relief grants and private-employment wage rates. The differentials shown are the differences between the midpoints of the relief and wage rate intervals. For example, cases with former relief grants ranging from $30 to $39 (midpoint $34.50) and private-employment wage rates ranging from $50 to $59 (midpoint $54.50) have been shown in the category Private-employment wage rates exceed relief grants by $20 a month.

Table 76.—Usual Occupational Group of Employed Workers, by Occupational Group of Works Program Employment at Time of Relief Closing and Race, 13 Cities, July—December 1935

Usual occupational group	Employed workers		Occupational group of Works Program employment					
			White-collar	Skilled	Semi-skilled	Unskilled		
	Number	Percent				Total	Manual	Domestic and personal service
ALL RACES[1]								
Experienced	140,563	100.0	5.5	3.6	8.1	82.8	82.4	0.4
White-collar	19,098	100.0	29.1	2.5	10.0	58.4	58.3	0.1
Skilled	21,532	100.0	3.4	15.8	2.1	78.7	78.7	*
Semiskilled	38,470	100.0	2.7	1.4	10.4	85.5	85.2	0.3
Unskilled	61,463	100.0	0.8	1.0	8.1	90.1	89.6	0.5
Manual	44,653	100.0	0.5	1.3	1.4	96.8	96.7	0.1
Domestic and personal service	16,810	100.0	1.5	0.3	26.2	72.0	70.3	1.7
Inexperienced	8,039	100.0	8.6	0.4	33.0	58.0	55.8	2.2
Unknown	179	100.0	5.0	0.6	8.4	86.0	82.1	3.9
WHITE								
Experienced	101,051	100.0	7.3	4.8	7.0	80.9	80.6	0.3
White-collar	16,749	100.0	31.5	2.7	10.7	55.1	55.0	0.1
Skilled	19,097	100.0	3.6	17.3	2.3	76.8	76.8	*
Semiskilled	30,651	100.0	3.4	1.5	9.3	85.8	85.6	0.2
Unskilled	34,554	100.0	1.0	1.8	5.8	91.4	90.8	0.6
Manual	27,676	100.0	0.7	2.1	1.9	95.3	95.3	*
Domestic and personal service	6,878	100.0	2.1	0.7	21.4	75.8	72.8	3.0
Inexperienced	6,367	100.0	10.2	0.5	32.2	57.1	55.4	1.7
Unknown	128	100.0	7.0	0.8	11.7	80.5	75.0	5.5
NEGRO								
Experienced	37,320	100.0	1.1	0.5	11.2	87.2	86.7	0.5
White-collar	2,253	100.0	12.0	0.8	5.1	82.1	81.9	0.2
Skilled	2,336	100.0	1.5	4.1	1.3	93.1	93.1	—
Semiskilled	7,489	100.0	0.2	0.6	14.5	84.7	83.6	1.1
Unskilled	25,242	100.0	0.5	0.1	11.6	87.8	87.4	0.4
Manual	15,720	100.0	0.1	0.1	0.2	99.6	99.5	0.1
Domestic and personal service	9,522	100.0	1.0	*	30.5	68.5	67.6	0.9
Inexperienced	1,575	100.0	2.1	—	36.1	61.8	57.2	4.6
Unknown	51	—	—	—	—	100.0	100.0	—

*Less than 0.05 percent.
[1]Includes "other" races.

Table 77.—Shift[1] From Usual Occupational Group by Employed Experienced Workers in Works Program Closings, by Race, 13 Cities, July—December 1935

Usual occupational group	Employed workers		Occupational shift[1]		
	Number	Percent	None	Upward	Downward
ALL RACES[2]					
Total	140,563	100.0	48.6	6.0	45.4
White-collar	19,098	100.0	29.1	([1])	70.9
Skilled	21,532	100.0	15.8	3.4	80.8
Semiskilled	38,470	100.0	10.4	4.1	85.5
Unskilled	61,463	100.0	90.1	9.9	([1])
WHITE					
Total	101,051	100.0	42.6	5.1	52.3
White-collar	16,749	100.0	31.5	([1])	68.5
Skilled	19,097	100.0	17.3	3.6	79.1
Semiskilled	30,651	100.0	9.3	4.9	85.8
Unskilled	34,554	100.0	91.4	8.6	([1])
NEGRO					
Total	37,320	100.0	63.3	8.5	28.2
White-collar	2,253	100.0	12.0	([1])	88.0
Skilled	2,336	100.0	4.1	1.5	94.4
Semiskilled	7,489	100.0	14.5	0.8	84.7
Unskilled	25,242	100.0	87.8	12.2	([1])

[1] 4 occupational groups are considered—white-collar, skilled, semiskilled, and unskilled. If a person's employment on the Works Program is in an occupational group other than his usual one, it is said that there was an "occupational shift." A shift toward the white-collar level has been termed an "upward shift," while a shift toward the unskilled level has been termed a "downward shift." By definition white-collar workers cannot shift upward and unskilled workers cannot shift downward.

[2] Includes "other" races.

Appendix B

LIST OF TABLES

141777 O—39——8